ECONOMICS FOR EVERYDAY LIFE

Elijah M. James, Ph. D.

Copyright © Elijah M. James

All rights reserved. No part of this book may be reproduced in any form or by any electronic or mechanical means, including information storage and retrieval systems without permission in writing from the author, except by a reviewer, who may quote brief passages in a review.

Canadian Cataloguing in Publication Data
James, Elijah M.
Economics for Everyday Life

ISBN 978-1-0690086-0-2

EJ Publishing
663 White Hills Run
Hammonds Plains
Nova Scotia, Canada. B4B 1W7

This book is lovingly dedicated to my cousin and dear friend Lem Martin and his wife Evan, who continue to inspire me to help improve people's lives.

Table of Contents

Preface 1
Acknowledgments 3

1. UNDERSTANDING ECONOMICS IN DAILY LIFE 5
The Basics of Economics 5
Why Economics Matters to Everyone 6
Dispelling Common Myths About Economics 7

2. INCOME AND EMPLOYMENT 10
Understanding Wages and Salaries 10
The Role of Income in Economic Decisions 11
Understanding Employment and Unemployment 13
The Impact of Wages on Spending Power 14

3. HOUSEHOLD ECONOMICS 17
Managing Household Budgets 17
The Economics of Family Decision-Making 19
Balancing Needs and Wants in a Household Setting 20

4. BUDGETING AND SPENDING 23
Creating a Personal Budget 23
Smart Spending 25
Saving for the Future 26

5. MAKING SENSE OF MONEY 29
The Role of Money in the Economy 29
How Inflation Impacts Everyday Life 31
Interest Rates and Their Influence on Spending 34

6. THE POWER OF MARKETS 38
Types of Markets: From Local to Global 38
How Markets Operate in Daily Life 41
The Role of Competition 44
Conclusion 48

7. SUPPLY AND DEMAND 49
The Law of Supply and Demand 49
Market Equilibrium: Where Supply Meets Demand 52
How Supply and Demand Affect Prices 55
Conclusion 57

8. THE ECONOMICS OF TIME MANAGEMENT 58
Valuing Time as an Economic Resource 58
Time Management Strategies for Maximizing Productivity ... 59
Balancing Work, Leisure, and Family Time 61
Conclusion 62

9. GOVERNMENT AND THE ECONOMY 63
Taxes and Public Services 63
Government Regulation and Its Impact 65
The Balance Between Free Markets and Government
Intervention 66
Conclusion 67

10. INVESTING AND GROWING WEALTH 69
Basics of Investing: Stocks, Bonds, and Real Estate 69
The Risk-Reward Trade-off 71
Planning for Retirement 72
Conclusion 74

11. ECONOMIC CYCLES AND YOU 75
Understanding Booms and Busts 75
How Economic Cycles Affect Employment and Spending 76
Preparing for Economic Uncertainty 76

12. GLOBAL ECONOMICS 78
The Impact of Global Trade on Daily Life 78
Currency Exchange and Its Effects 80
How Global Events Influence Local Economies 81
Conclusion 83

13. CONSUMER BEHAVIOUR AND DECISION-MAKING 85
The Psychology Behind Spending Choices 85
Factors That Influence Consumer Decisions 88
The Impact of Advertising on Buying Habits 91
Conclusion 95

14. THE ROLE OF TECHNOLOGY IN THE ECONOMY 97
How Technological Advancements Affect Employment 97
The Rise of E-Commerce and Its Impact on Traditional Markets 99
The Future of Work in a Digital Age 100
Conclusion 101

15. THE DIGITAL ECONOMY 102
The Growth of the Digital Marketplace 102
Cryptocurrency and Digital Payments 103
The Impact of Digitalization on Traditional Industries 105
Conclusion 106

16. HEALTHCARE ECONOMICS 107
The Cost of Healthcare and Its Economic Impact 107
Understanding Health Insurance 108
The Role of Government in Healthcare 110
Conclusion 111

17. HOUSING AND REAL ESTATE 113
The Economics of Buying vs. Renting 113
Understanding Mortgages and Interest Rates 115
The Impact of the Housing Market on the Economy 116
Conclusion 118

18. THE ECONOMICS OF EDUCATION 119
The Cost of Education and Its Return on Investment 119
Student Loans and Financial Aid 121
The Role of Education in Economic Mobility 123
Conclusion 124

19. ENVIRONMENTAL ECONOMICS 126
The Economic Impact of Environmental Policies 126
The Cost of Sustainable Practices 128
Balancing Economic Growth with Environmental
Responsibility 130
Conclusion 132

20. MAKING INFORMED ECONOMIC DECISIONS . 133
How to Analyze Economic Data 133
Understanding Economic Indicators 134
Applying Economic Principles to Everyday Decisions 135

21. RETIREMENT PLANNING AND SOCIAL SECURITY 138
Understanding Social Security Benefits 138
Planning for Retirement: Saving Strategies and Investment Options 139
The Future of Retirement in an Aging Society 141

22. THE FUTURE OF WORK 143
The Rise of Remote and Gig Work 143
The Impact of Automation and AI on Employment 145
Preparing for the Workforce of the Future 146
Conclusion 147

23. THE FUTURE OF THE ECONOMY 148
Emerging Trends in Technology and Business 148
The Gig Economy and Its Impact on Employment 150
Preparing for Economic Changes in the Future 151
Conclusion 152

APPENDIX 153
GLOSSARY OF ECONOMIC TERMS 155

Preface

In a world that is increasingly interconnected and fast-paced, the role of economics in our daily lives has never been more significant. Whether we realize it or not, economic principles influence nearly every decision we make— from the groceries we buy to the savings we set aside for the future, to the policies that govern our communities and nations. Yet, for many, the world of economics can seem daunting and abstract, reserved only for experts and analysts.

This book, *Economics for Everyday Life*, is born out of the belief that economics is not just for the classroom or the boardroom; it is a vital part of everyday living that everyone can understand and apply. My goal in writing this book is to demystify economics and show how its principles are woven into the fabric of our daily lives. I want to provide you with the tools and knowledge to make informed decisions that will improve your financial well-being and give you greater confidence in navigating the economic forces around you.

Throughout this book, we will explore key economic concepts in a way that is clear, relatable, and practical. You don't need a background in economics to benefit from this journey. Whether you are a student, a professional, a retiree, or anyone in between, this book is designed to meet you where you are, offering insights that are directly applicable to your life.

The chapters ahead will guide you through the basics of supply and demand, the impact of inflation, the importance of personal financial management, and much more. By the end of this book, my hope is that you will see economics not as a distant or complex field, but as a set of tools that can empower you to make better choices, achieve your goals, and enhance your quality of life.

Economics, at its core, is about people—how we interact, how we allocate scarce resources, and how we strive to improve our lives and the lives of those around us. This book is an invitation to view the world through an economic lens, with the assurance that doing so will enrich your understanding of the world and your place within it.

Thank you for choosing to embark on this journey with me. I hope you find the lessons within these pages as enlightening and empowering as I have found in bringing them to you.

Acknowledgments

Writing *Economics for Everyday Life* has been a deeply fulfilling journey, one that has brought together my passion for economics and my commitment to making complex ideas accessible to everyone. This book would not have been possible without the support, encouragement, and contributions of many individuals, to whom I owe my deepest gratitude.

First and foremost, I would like to thank my family, whose unwavering support has been the foundation upon which this project was built. Your patience, understanding, and belief in my work have sustained me through the long hours of research and writing.

I am also profoundly grateful to my mentors and colleagues in the field of economics, whose insights and feedback have enriched this book in countless ways. Your willingness to share your knowledge and challenge my thinking has pushed me to produce a work that I hope will make a meaningful impact.

A special thank you goes to my editor, whose keen eye and thoughtful suggestions have helped shape this book into a clearer and more engaging read. Your expertise and dedication have been invaluable throughout this process.

To the readers and students who have inspired this book—whether through your curiosity, your questions, or your desire to understand the world around you—I extend my heartfelt thanks. It is for you that this book was written, and I hope it serves as a helpful guide in your own journeys.

Lastly, I would like to acknowledge the countless individuals who work tirelessly behind the scenes to bring a book to life, from the publishing team to the designers and marketers. Your efforts are deeply appreciated and have made this book a reality.

To everyone who has contributed to the creation of *Economics for Everyday Life*, I am deeply thankful. This book is as much a product of your support as it is of my own efforts, and I am honoured to share it with the world.

1.
UNDERSTANDING ECONOMICS IN DAILY LIFE

The Basics of Economics

At its core, economics is the study of how individuals, businesses, governments, and societies allocate limited resources to satisfy their unlimited wants and needs. It's about making choices—how we decide what to buy, what to save, where to invest, and how to manage our time and money effectively. These choices are influenced by the scarcity of resources, the costs and benefits associated with different options, and the incentives that guide our behaviour.

Economics can be broadly divided into two main branches: microeconomics and macroeconomics. Microeconomics focuses on the behaviour of individuals and businesses, examining how they make decisions and how these decisions interact in markets. Topics like supply and demand, pricing, and consumer behaviour all fall under the umbrella of microeconomics.

Macroeconomics, on the other hand, looks at the economy as a whole. It studies large-scale economic factors such as inflation, unemployment, economic growth, and monetary policy. While microeconomics might explain why the price of coffee has increased at your local café, macroeconomics would help you understand how national policies or global economic trends are influencing those prices.

Understanding these basic concepts is the first step in recognizing how economics influences every aspect of our lives. From the groceries you buy to the interest rates on your mortgage, economic principles are at work, shaping your decisions and the outcomes of those decisions.

Why Economics Matters to Everyone

You might wonder why economics should matter to you if you're not an economist or a businessperson. The truth is, economics is relevant to everyone because it impacts every facet of our daily lives. Whether you're managing your household budget, planning for retirement, deciding on a career, or voting in an election, economic principles play a crucial role in guiding your choices.

For instance, consider the concept of opportunity cost, which is the value of the next best alternative that you forgo when making a decision. Every time you make a choice, you're incurring an opportunity cost, whether it's choosing to spend money on a vacation instead of saving it for the future, or deciding to spend time with family instead of working overtime. Understanding opportunity costs helps you make more informed decisions by considering not just what you're gaining, but also what you're giving up.

Another key concept is the idea of incentives. Incentives are factors that motivate individuals and businesses to behave in certain ways. Governments use incentives like tax breaks to encourage people to buy homes or start businesses, while companies use incentives like discounts and loyalty programs to attract and retain customers. By understanding how incentives work, you can better navigate the choices presented to you and even use them to your advantage.

Economics also plays a critical role in understanding and addressing broader societal issues such as inequality, poverty, and environmental sustainability. For example, economic policies can either exacerbate or alleviate income inequality, depending on how they're designed and implemented. Similarly, economic tools can be used to promote sustainable practices and address climate change by creating incentives for businesses and consumers to reduce their environmental footprint.

In essence, economics provides a framework for understanding the world around us. It helps us make sense of the complex interactions between individuals, businesses, and governments, and equips us with the tools to make better decisions in our personal and professional lives.

Dispelling Common Myths About Economics

Despite its importance, economics is often misunderstood, leading to several common myths that can create unnecessary fear or confusion. Let's address a few of these myths to clarify what economics is—and isn't.

Myth 1: Economics is Just About Money

One of the most pervasive myths is that economics is solely concerned with money. While money is certainly a central theme, economics is much broader. It's about the allocation of all types of resources—time, labour, materials, and even social capital (relationships among people that contribute to the success of an undertaking). Economics examines how we use these resources to achieve various goals, whether it's producing goods, providing services, or enhancing well-being.

Myth 2: Economics is Only for Experts

Another common misconception is that economics is too complicated for the average person to understand. While economics does involve technical concepts and mathematical models, its fundamental principles are accessible to everyone. You don't need a degree in economics to understand the basics of supply and demand, inflation, or budgeting. In fact, this book is designed to show you how these concepts apply to your daily life in practical ways.

Myth 3: Economics is About Predicting the Future

While economics can provide insights into trends and help forecast future outcomes, it is not a crystal ball. Economists use data, models, and historical analysis to make informed predictions, but these predictions are always subject to uncertainty. Economic outcomes are influenced by a wide range of factors, including human behaviour, which can be unpredictable. Therefore, economics is more about understanding possibilities and probabilities than making definitive predictions.

Myth 4: Economics is a Dismal Science

Economics has sometimes been labeled as the "dismal science," a term coined in the 19th century because of the often pessimistic predictions made by early economists. However, economics is far from dismal. It is a dynamic and evolving field that seeks to understand and improve the way we live. By applying economic principles, we can find innovative solutions to some of the world's most pressing problems, from poverty and inequality to environmental sustainability.

By dispelling these myths, we can better appreciate the value of economics in our lives. Economics is not just about numbers and graphs; it's about understanding human behaviour, making informed choices, and striving to create a better world for ourselves and future generations.

In this first chapter, we've explored the basics of economics, why it matters to everyone, and debunked some common myths that might have deterred you from engaging with the subject. As we move forward, we'll dive deeper into how these economic principles play out in various aspects of everyday life, equipping you with the knowledge and confidence to make informed decisions that will enhance your financial well-being and overall quality of life.

2.
INCOME AND EMPLOYMENT

Understanding Wages and Salaries

Wages and salaries are fundamental components of personal income and play a crucial role in the economy. They represent the compensation individuals receive in exchange for their labour, skills, and time. Understanding the distinction between wages and salaries is essential to grasp how income is generated and how it impacts daily life.

Wages

Wages are typically paid on an hourly basis. This means that an employee's income fluctuates depending on the number of hours worked. For example, a worker paid $15 per hour who works 40 hours a week will earn $600. Wages are common in jobs that require manual labour, such as construction, retail, or service industry positions.

Salaries

Salaries, on the other hand, are usually expressed as an annual sum but are paid out periodically, such as monthly or biweekly. Salaried employees earn a fixed amount regardless of the number of hours worked. This type of compensation is more common in professional and managerial positions. For instance, an employee with an annual salary of $50,000 will receive regular payments divided across the year, providing a stable and predictable income.

Both wages and salaries are influenced by various factors, including the industry, the level of skill required, education, experience, and geographic location. Understanding these elements helps individuals make informed decisions about their careers and financial planning.

The Role of Income in Economic Decisions

Income is at the heart of economic decision-making, influencing how individuals and households allocate their resources. The amount of income one earns directly impacts his or her ability to meet basic needs, save for the future, and enjoy discretionary spending. The role of income in economic decisions can be seen in several areas:

Budgeting:

Income dictates the scope of a household budget. Individuals must balance their earnings with their expenses, making choices about how to allocate funds for necessities such as housing, food, transportation, and healthcare. Discretionary spending on entertainment, travel, or luxury items is determined by the surplus income after meeting essential needs.

Saving and Investing

Income levels influence an individual's capacity to save and invest. Higher income often allows for greater savings, which can be invested to grow wealth over time. Conversely, those with lower incomes may struggle to save, prioritizing immediate needs over long-term financial goals.

Borrowing and Debt Management

Income also plays a critical role in borrowing decisions. Lenders assess individuals' income to determine their ability to repay loans. A stable, sufficient income can provide access to credit for major purchases, such as a home or car. However, inadequate income may lead to higher interest rates or loan rejections, making debt management more challenging.

Consumption Choices

The level of income affects consumption patterns, determining the quality and quantity of goods and services one can afford. For example, higher-income individuals may opt for organic foods, private education, or high-end electronics, while those with lower incomes may choose more cost-effective alternatives.

Understanding the role of income in economic decisions empowers individuals to make informed choices that align with their financial goals and personal values.

Understanding Employment and Unemployment

Employment is a vital component of the economy, providing individuals with the means to earn income and support themselves and their families. The employment landscape is shaped by various factors, including the demand for labour, technological advancements, and economic policies.

Employment

Employment refers to the state of having a job or being engaged in work that provides income. It encompasses full-time, part-time, and self-employment. Full-time employment typically offers more stability and benefits, such as health insurance and retirement plans, while part-time work may provide flexibility but often lacks these benefits. Part-time employment may be used as a means of supplementing income from full-time employment.

Unemployment

Unemployment occurs when individuals who are willing and able to work cannot find employment. Unemployment can have significant personal and societal impacts, including financial hardship, increased reliance on social welfare programs, and reduced economic productivity.

Types of Unemployment

There are several types of unemployment:

Frictional Unemployment: This occurs when individuals are temporarily out of work while transitioning between jobs. It is a natural part of the labour market as people move to new locations, change careers, or seek better opportunities.

Structural Unemployment: This arises when there is a mismatch between the skills workers possess and the skills demanded by employers. Technological changes, shifts in consumer preferences, or globalization can contribute to structural unemployment, as certain industries decline while others grow.

Cyclical Unemployment: This type of unemployment is linked to the economic cycle. During a recession, demand for goods and services decreases, leading to job losses. Conversely, during economic expansion, demand increases, and unemployment typically decreases.

Seasonal Unemployment: Some industries, such as agriculture or tourism, experience fluctuations in demand based on the season. Workers in these industries may face unemployment during off-peak periods.

Understanding employment and unemployment helps individuals navigate the job market and make informed decisions about their careers. It also highlights the importance of education and skill development in maintaining employability in a rapidly changing economy.

The Impact of Wages on Spending Power

Wages directly influence individuals' spending power, which refers to their ability to purchase goods and services. The higher the wages, the greater the spending power, allowing individuals to afford a higher standard of living. Conversely, low wages limit spending power, often forcing individuals to prioritize essential needs and cut back on discretionary spending.

Spending power is affected by several factors:

Inflation: As prices for goods and services rise, the purchasing power of wages declines. Even if wages increase nominally, if they do not keep pace with inflation, the real value of income diminishes, reducing spending power.

Taxes: The amount of income that individuals can actually spend is affected by taxation. Higher taxes reduce disposable income, while tax cuts can increase it. Understanding tax obligations and potential deductions is important for maximizing spending power.

Location: Geographic location plays a significant role in spending power. In areas with a high cost of living, such as major cities, even higher wages may not translate into greater spending power owing to the higher prices of housing, food, and other essentials. Conversely, in areas with a lower cost of living, lower wages may still provide substantial spending power.

Debt: The burden of debt payments can significantly reduce spending power. Individuals with high levels of debt may find that a large portion of their income is devoted to servicing loans, leaving less available for other expenses.

Understanding the impact of wages on spending power is crucial for making informed financial decisions. It allows individuals to plan their budgets effectively, manage their debt, and make strategic choices about where to live and work.

This chapter has explored the complex relationship between income, employment, and economic decisions. By understanding these elements, individuals can better navigate their financial lives, making informed choices that lead to greater stability and prosperity.

3.
HOUSEHOLD ECONOMICS

Managing Household Budgets

Managing a household budget is one of the most critical aspects of household economics. A well-planned budget serves as a financial roadmap, helping families allocate resources, meet financial obligations, and achieve their goals. Understanding the basics of budgeting and the strategies for effective management can significantly enhance a household's financial stability.

Creating a Budget

The first step in managing a household budget is creating one. One cannot manage something that does not exist. This involves listing all sources of income, including wages, salaries, and any additional earnings, and then categorizing expenses into essential and non-essential items. Essential expenses include housing, utilities, food, transportation, and healthcare. Non-essential expenses might include dining out, entertainment, and hobbies.

Tracking Expenses

To manage a budget effectively, it's crucial to track spending. This can be done manually with a ledger or by using budgeting apps that categorize and analyze spending patterns. By closely monitoring where money goes, households can identify areas where they may be overspending and adjust their habits accordingly.

Saving and Emergency Funds

A key component of household budgeting is setting aside money for savings and emergencies. Financial experts often recommend having an emergency fund covering three to six months' expenses. This fund can provide a cushion in case of unexpected events like job loss, medical emergencies, or major home repairs.

Debt Management

For many households, managing debt is an essential part of budgeting. Prioritizing debt repayment, especially high-interest debt, can free up future income for savings and investments. Strategies like the debt snowball (paying off the smallest debts as fast as possible) or the avalanche method (paying off the loan with the highest interest rate first) can be effective in reducing debt over time.

Adjusting the Budget

A budget is not static; it should be adjusted as circumstances change. Whether it's an increase in income, the birth of a child, or an unexpected medical expense, households should regularly review and revise their budgets to ensure they continue to meet their needs.

The Economics of Family Decision-Making

Family decision-making often involves complex economic considerations. Unlike individual decision-making, family economics requires balancing the needs and desires of multiple people with their own priorities and preferences. Understanding the dynamics of family decision-making can help households make choices that benefit everyone involved.

Collective Decision-Making

In a family, decisions about spending, saving, and investing are often made collectively. This process requires open communication, where all members can express their opinions and preferences. It's important to consider the needs of the entire household, including children when making financial decisions. This collective approach ensures that decisions reflect the family's overall goals and values.

Setting Financial Goals

Establishing shared financial goals is a cornerstone of family economics. Whether saving for a family vacation, a child's education, or retirement, setting goals helps guide financial decisions. It's important to ensure that these goals are realistic and achievable, taking into account the family's income, expenses, and long-term plans.

Negotiating and Compromising:

Family decision-making often involves negotiation and compromise. For example, one family member might prioritize saving for a new car, while another might want to renovate the kitchen. Balancing these competing desires requires finding a middle ground that satisfies everyone's needs. Compromise is essential in maintaining harmony within the household and ensuring that financial decisions are made with everyone's best interests in mind.

Long-Term Planning

Effective family decision-making also involves long-term planning. Families need to consider future expenses, such as college tuition, healthcare costs, and retirement. Planning for these long-term needs requires a forward-looking approach, where current spending is balanced with future financial security.

Involving Children in Financial Decisions

Teaching children about money management from a young age can be a valuable part of family decision-making. Involving children in discussions about budgeting, saving, and spending can help them develop strong financial habits that will benefit them in adulthood.

Balancing Needs and Wants in a Household Setting

One of the most challenging aspects of household economics is balancing needs and wants. While needs are essential for survival and well-being, wants are often driven by desire and personal preference. Understanding how to balance these two can lead to better financial health and greater satisfaction within the household.

Identifying Needs and Wants

The first step in balancing needs and wants is identifying which expenses fall into each category. Needs are the essentials—food, shelter, clothing, healthcare, and education. Wants, on the other hand, are things that enhance the quality of life but are not necessary for survival, such as dining out, entertainment, and luxury items.

Prioritizing Needs

In any household budget, needs must be prioritized. Ensuring that essential expenses are covered before allocating money to wants is critical. This means paying the mortgage or rent, utility bills, and grocery expenses before spending on non-essential items.

Making Conscious Spending Choices

Balancing needs and wants requires making conscious spending choices. This involves evaluating whether a purchase is necessary or if the money could be better spent elsewhere. For example, rather than dining out frequently, a family might choose to cook at home more often to save money for a family vacation.

It's important to set limits on spending for wants. This can be done by allocating a specific portion of the budget to discretionary spending. For example, a household might decide that 10% of the monthly budget can be spent on entertainment, hobbies, or dining out. Setting these limits helps prevent overspending and ensures that financial resources are used wisely.

Finding Joy in Simplicity

Finally, balancing needs and wants often involves finding joy in simplicity. This might mean prioritizing experiences over material goods or finding contentment in what the family already has. By focusing on the things that truly matter—relationships, health, and well-being—households can reduce the emphasis on material wants and find greater satisfaction in their financial choices.

In this chapter, we've explored the complexities of household economics, from managing budgets to making collective decisions and balancing needs and wants. By understanding these concepts, households can make informed financial decisions that promote stability, satisfaction, and long-term prosperity.

4.
BUDGETING AND SPENDING

Creating a Personal Budget

Creating a personal budget is the foundation of sound financial management. It's a strategic plan for how you'll allocate your income to meet your expenses, achieve your financial goals, and prepare for the future. A well-crafted budget allows you to take control of your finances, avoid debt, and build wealth over time.

Understanding Your Income and Expenses

The first step in creating a budget is to understand your income and expenses. Begin by listing all sources of income, including your salary, freelance work, side businesses, investments, and any other earnings. Next, track your expenses for a month to get a clear picture of where your money is going. Categorize your expenses into fixed costs (such as rent, utilities, and loan payments) and variable costs (such as groceries, entertainment, and dining out).

Setting Financial Goals

Your budget should be aligned with your financial goals, whether short-term (like saving for a vacation) or long-term (like buying a home or retiring comfortably). Setting specific, measurable, achievable, relevant, and time-bound (SMART) goals will help you stay focused and motivated. For instance, if you want to save $10,000 for a down payment on a house in two years, you'll need to set aside about $417 per month.

Allocating Your Income

Once you've identified your income, expenses, and financial goals, it's time to allocate your income accordingly. A popular budgeting rule is the 50/30/20 rule, which suggests that 50% of your income should go toward needs, 30% toward wants, and 20% toward savings and debt repayment. However, you can adjust these percentages based on your specific situation and goals.

Tracking and Adjusting Your Budget

A budget isn't static; it needs to be tracked and adjusted regularly. Use budgeting apps, spreadsheets, or even a simple notebook to record your expenses and compare them to your budget. If you're consistently overspending in certain categories, consider making adjustments. Similarly, if your income increases, revisit your budget to allocate the additional funds toward your goals.

Avoiding Common Budgeting Pitfalls

Many people struggle with budgeting because they make it too complicated or unrealistic. Start simple and be honest about your spending habits. Another common mistake is not accounting for irregular expenses, such as car repairs or medical bills. Include a buffer in your budget for these unpredictable costs. Finally, don't forget to reward yourself occasionally to stay motivated—just be sure it's within your budget!

Smart Spending

Making smart spending decisions that align with your financial goals is extremely important.

Making Conscious Spending Choices

Being mindful of your spending is a key component of smart financial management. Before making a purchase, ask yourself if it's a need or a want, and whether it fits into your budget. This doesn't mean you can never indulge in wants, but it does mean making conscious choices that align with your financial priorities. For instance, you might choose to cook at home more often so that you can save for a vacation or pay down debt faster.

Using Cash or Debit Instead of Credit

One effective strategy for controlling spending on wants is to use cash or a debit card instead of a credit card. This helps you avoid overspending and accumulating debt. If you're using a credit card, be sure to pay off the balance in full each month to avoid interest charges.

The Envelope System

The envelope system is a budgeting technique that can help you manage your spending on wants. Allocate a specific amount of cash for discretionary spending (like dining out, entertainment, and shopping) and place it in an envelope. Once the cash is gone, you can't spend any more in that category until the next budgeting period. This method forces you to stick to your budget and prioritize your spending.

The Importance of Balance

While it's important to control spending on wants, it's also essential to find a balance that allows you to enjoy life. Depriving yourself completely can lead to frustration and burnout. Instead, allocate a portion of your budget to wants, but keep it within limits that won't jeopardize your financial goals.

Saving for the Future

Saving is a critical component of any budget. It provides a safety net for unexpected expenses, allows you to achieve your financial goals, and ensures a secure future. But saving requires discipline and a clear plan.

The Importance of Saving

Saving money is essential for financial security and peace of mind. It allows you to handle unexpected expenses, such as car repairs or medical bills, without going into debt. It also provides the funds you need to achieve your goals, such as buying a home, traveling, or retiring comfortably. Without savings, you may find yourself living from paycheck to paycheck, with little room for financial emergencies or opportunities.

Types of Savings

There are several types of savings that you should consider, each serving a different purpose:

Emergency Fund: An emergency fund is a cash reserve set aside for unexpected expenses. Some financial experts recommend having three to six months' worth of living expenses in an easily accessible account, such as a savings or money market account.

Short-Term Savings: Short-term savings are funds set aside for expenses you expect to incur within the next few years, such as a vacation, a new car, or home improvements. These funds should be kept in a liquid account, where they can earn interest but still be accessible when needed.

Long-Term Savings: Long-term savings are for goals that are several years or even decades away, such as buying a home, funding your children's education, or retiring. These funds are often invested in stocks, bonds, or retirement accounts, where they can grow over time.

Paying Yourself First: A key strategy for successful saving is to "pay yourself first." This means treating savings as a non-negotiable expense, just like rent or utilities. Set up automatic transfers to your savings account as soon as you receive your paycheck, so you're saving consistently without having to think about it.

Budgeting for Savings: Your budget should include a line item for savings. Aim to save at least 20% of your income, if possible. If you're not able to save this much right away, start with a smaller percentage and gradually increase it over time. Prioritize building your emergency fund first, then focus on short-term and long-term savings goals.

The Power of Compound Interest: One of the most powerful tools in saving for the future is compound interest. This is the interest you earn on both your initial savings and the interest that accumulates over time. The earlier you start saving, the more you can benefit from compound interest, as your money has more time to grow. Even small contributions can grow significantly over time, especially if you invest in accounts with higher interest rates or returns. Remember though, that higher interest rates often mean greater risk.

Saving for Retirement: Retirement may seem far off, but the sooner you start saving for it, the better off you'll be. Take advantage of retirement accounts like 401(k)s or IRAs, which offer tax advantages and often include employer contributions. Aim to save at least 15% of your income for retirement, and increase this amount as your income grows.

Overcoming Saving Challenges: Saving can be challenging, especially if you're living on a tight budget. But it's important to remember that even small amounts add up over time. Look for ways to reduce expenses, increase income, or find extra money to put toward savings. Avoid lifestyle inflation, where your spending increases as your income grows, and prioritize saving any extra income.

In this chapter, we've explored the essential aspects of budgeting and spending, from creating a personal budget to making smart spending decisions and saving for the future. By mastering these skills, you can achieve greater financial security, meet your goals, and enjoy a more balanced and fulfilling life.

5.
MAKING SENSE OF MONEY

The Role of Money in the Economy

Let us begin by defining money. Money is anything that is generally accepted as final payment for goods or services.

Money is the lifeblood of the economy, serving as a medium of exchange, a unit of account, a store of value, and a standard of deferred payment. Understanding its role is crucial to making informed financial decisions in both personal and broader economic contexts.

Medium of Exchange

Money facilitates transactions by eliminating the inefficiencies of barter, where goods and services are directly exchanged for other goods and services. In a barter system, the problem of a "double coincidence of wants" arises—both parties must have something the other wants. Money solves this by providing a universally accepted medium of exchange, allowing people to sell goods or services for money and use that money to purchase what they want from others.

Unit of Account

Money serves as a common measure of value, making it easier to compare the worth of different goods and services. By expressing prices in terms of a monetary unit, such as dollars, people can easily understand and compare the cost of items, enabling them to make informed purchasing decisions. This standardization also simplifies accounting and record-keeping, as all transactions can be recorded in the same unit of measure. The unit of account is also referred to as a *measure of value*.

Store of Value

Money allows people to save purchasing power for the future. Unlike perishable goods, which may lose value over time, money can be saved and used later without losing its value (assuming inflation is under control). This feature of money enables individuals to plan for the future, save for large purchases, or build a financial cushion for emergencies. Obviously, money is not a good store of value during periods of high inflation because it loses purchasing power.

Standard of Deferred Payment

Money is used to settle debts and is accepted in transactions where payment is deferred, such as loans or installment plans. This role of money is critical in modern economies, where credit plays a significant role. When you take out a loan, you agree to pay back the amount borrowed plus interest in the future, and money serves as the standard for these future payments.

The Evolution of Money

Over time, money has evolved from commodity money (such as gold and silver) to fiat money (currency without intrinsic value but established as money by government regulation). Today, money takes various forms, including physical currency, digital currencies, and electronic payments, all of which facilitate the functioning of the global economy.

Money and Economic Stability

Central banks, such as the Federal Reserve in the United States, the Bank of Canada, and the Bank of England, play a crucial role in maintaining the stability of the monetary system. By controlling the money supply, setting interest rates, and regulating financial institutions, central banks influence inflation, employment, and economic growth. Understanding how money operates in the economy helps individuals and businesses navigate economic cycles and make better financial decisions.

How Inflation Impacts Everyday Life

Inflation is the rate at which the general level of prices for goods and services rises, eroding purchasing power. While a moderate level of inflation is normal in a growing economy, high or unpredictable inflation can have significant effects on everyday life.

Understanding Inflation

Inflation occurs when the quantity of goods and services demanded exceeds the quantity supplied, or when the cost of production (such as wages and raw materials) increases. Central banks monitor inflation closely and use monetary policy tools, such as interest rates, to keep inflation within a target range. In the U.S., for example, the Federal Reserve aims for an inflation rate of around 2% annually.

The Erosion of Purchasing Power

As prices rise, the purchasing power of money decreases, meaning that a dollar buys less today than it did in the past. This erosion of purchasing power affects everyone, but it hits those on fixed incomes, such as retirees, the hardest. For example, if the inflation rate is 3% per year, something that costs $100 today will cost $103 next year. Over time, even small inflation rates can significantly reduce the value of savings.

Wage Growth and Inflation

Ideally, wages should rise in line with inflation to maintain purchasing power. However, this is not always the case. If wages stagnate while prices rise, workers find it more difficult to afford basic necessities, leading to a decrease in their standard of living. On the other hand, if wages increase faster than inflation, it can lead to higher demand for goods and services, potentially fueling further inflation.

Impact on Savings and Investments

Inflation can erode the value of savings, particularly if the interest earned on savings accounts is lower than the inflation rate. For example, if you have a savings account with an interest rate of 1% and inflation is 2%, the real value of your savings is actually decreasing. To protect against inflation, investors often seek assets that provide higher returns, such as stocks, real estate, or inflation-protected securities.

The Cost of Borrowing

Inflation affects interest rates, which in turn influences the cost of borrowing money. During periods of high inflation, central banks may raise interest rates to cool down the economy, making loans more expensive for consumers and businesses. Higher interest rates increase the cost of mortgages, car loans, and credit card debt, which can reduce consumer spending and slow economic growth.

Inflation and Consumer Behaviour

High inflation can lead to changes in consumer behaviour. As prices rise, people may cut back on discretionary spending, delay big purchases, or seek out lower-cost alternatives. In extreme cases, if people expect prices to keep rising rapidly, they may start hoarding goods, which can lead to shortages and further price increases.

Hyperinflation and Its Consequences

In rare cases, economies experience hyperinflation, where prices increase rapidly and uncontrollably, often due to a collapse in the value of the currency. Hyperinflation can lead to severe economic disruption, social unrest, and the collapse of the financial system, as seen in historical examples like Zimbabwe in the 2000s or Germany in the 1920s.

Interest Rates and Their Influence on Spending

Interest rates play a central role in the economy, influencing everything from consumer spending to business investment and government policy. Understanding how interest rates work and their impact on spending is essential for making informed financial decisions.

What Are Interest Rates?

Interest rates represent the cost of borrowing money or the return on savings. They are expressed as a percentage of the principal (the amount borrowed or saved) and can be fixed or variable. Central banks set short-term interest rates, which influence other interest rates in the economy, including those on mortgages, car loans, and savings accounts.

The Relationship Between Interest Rates and Economic Activity

Interest rates are a powerful tool used by central banks to manage economic activity. When the economy is growing too quickly and inflation is rising, central banks may increase interest rates to cool down spending and investment. Conversely, when the economy is sluggish and unemployment is high, central banks may lower interest rates to encourage borrowing and spending.

Impact on Consumer Spending

Interest rates directly affect consumer spending, particularly on big-ticket items that are often financed through loans, such as homes, cars, and appliances. When interest rates are low, borrowing is cheaper, encouraging consumers to take out loans and make purchases. This increased spending can stimulate economic growth. On the other hand, when interest rates rise, the cost of borrowing increases, leading to reduced consumer spending and a slowdown in economic activity.

Mortgage Rates and Housing Market

Interest rates have a significant impact on the housing market. Lower interest rates make mortgages more affordable, leading to increased demand for homes and higher property prices. Conversely, higher interest rates make mortgages more expensive, reducing demand and potentially leading to a decline in housing prices. For homeowners with adjustable-rate mortgages, changes in interest rates can directly affect their monthly payments, making it crucial to consider interest rate trends when buying a home.

Savings and Investment Returns

Interest rates also influence the returns on savings and investments. When interest rates are high, savings accounts and fixed-income investments, such as bonds, offer better returns, encouraging people to save more. However, when interest rates are low, the return on savings diminishes, prompting investors to seek higher returns in riskier assets, such as stocks or real estate.

Business Investment and Economic Growth

Interest rates affect businesses' decisions to invest in new projects, expand operations, or hire additional staff.

When interest rates are low, borrowing costs are reduced, making it more attractive for businesses to take out loans and invest in growth. This can lead to increased production, job creation, and economic expansion. However, when interest rates rise, the cost of financing increases, which can deter investment and slow down economic growth.

Government Borrowing and Fiscal Policy

Interest rates also impact government borrowing and fiscal policy. When interest rates are low, governments can borrow more cheaply to finance public projects, social programs, or deficit spending. However, high interest rates increase the cost of servicing government debt, which can lead to higher taxes or reduced public spending. Central banks must carefully balance interest rates to support economic growth while keeping inflation in check.

Global Interest Rate Trends

In today's interconnected global economy, interest rate changes in one country can have ripple effects worldwide. For example, suppose the U.S. Federal Reserve raises interest rates. In that case, it can attract foreign investors seeking higher returns, leading to a stronger U.S. dollar and affecting international trade and investment flows. Understanding global interest rate trends can help individuals and businesses make informed decisions about cross-border investments and currency risks.

In this chapter, we've explored the fundamental concepts of money, inflation, and interest rates, and their impact on the economy and individual financial decisions. By understanding these concepts, you can navigate the complexities of the financial world with greater confidence and make informed choices that support your economic well-being.

6.
THE POWER OF MARKETS

Types of Markets: From Local to Global

Markets are the arenas where buyers and sellers come together to exchange goods, services, and resources. They exist in various forms, from small local markets to vast global networks, each playing a crucial role in the economy. Understanding the different types of markets helps us appreciate their influence on our daily lives.

Local Markets

Local markets are small-scale markets typically found in towns, cities, and neighbourhoods. They include farmers' markets, flea markets, and local shops where goods and services are exchanged within a specific community. Local markets are often characterized by direct interactions between buyers and sellers, fostering personal relationships and a sense of community. They are vital for small businesses and local economies, providing opportunities for entrepreneurship and the circulation of money within the community.

Regional Markets

Regional markets encompass a broader geographical area, including multiple cities or regions. These markets often involve larger-scale operations, such as regional retail chains, agricultural markets, or regional trade fairs. Regional markets benefit from economies of scale, allowing businesses to reach a wider audience while still maintaining some level of direct interaction with consumers. They play a critical role in distributing goods and services across a region, ensuring that products from different areas are accessible to consumers.

National Markets

National markets cover the entire country, integrating local and regional markets into a single, cohesive market. These markets are often dominated by larger corporations, retail chains, and service providers with a nationwide presence. National markets benefit from uniform regulations, standards, and currency, which facilitate trade and commerce across the country. They are essential for the distribution of goods and services on a large scale, ensuring that consumers across the nation have access to a wide range of products.

Global Markets

Global markets are vast networks of trade that span across multiple countries and continents. They are characterized by international trade, investment, and the exchange of goods, services, and capital across borders. Global markets are driven by advancements in technology, transportation, and communication, enabling businesses to operate and compete on a global scale. These markets are critical for the global economy, promoting economic growth, innovation, and cultural exchange. However, they also introduce complexities such as currency fluctuations, trade regulations, and geopolitical risks.

Digital Markets

With the rise of the internet and digital technologies, digital markets have become increasingly important. These markets operate online, allowing buyers and sellers to interact in virtual spaces. E-commerce platforms, online marketplaces, and digital services have transformed the way we shop, work, and interact with the economy. Digital markets offer convenience, a vast selection of products, and global reach, but they also raise concerns about data privacy, cybersecurity, and the digital divide.

Specialized Markets

In addition to general markets, there are specialized markets that cater to specific industries or products. Examples include financial markets (such as stock exchanges and bond markets), real estate markets, labour markets, and commodity markets. Each of these markets operates under its own set of rules, regulations, and dynamics, and they play a vital role in the functioning of the broader economy.

How Markets Operate in Daily Life

Markets are not just abstract economic concepts—they are an integral part of our everyday lives, influencing the choices we make, the prices we pay, and the availability of goods and services.

Supply and Demand

At the core of any market is the principle of supply and demand. Supply refers to the various quantities of a product or service that sellers are willing to make available at various prices. Demand, on the other hand, refers to the various quantities of a product or service that buyers are willing and able to purchase at various prices. The interaction between supply and demand determines the price of goods and services in the market. When the quantity demanded exceeds the quantity supplied, the price tends to rise, and when the quantity supplied exceeds the quantity demanded, the price tends to fall. Understanding this basic principle helps us navigate the fluctuations in prices and availability that we encounter in our daily lives.

Price Signals

Prices in the market act as signals to both buyers and sellers. For consumers, prices indicate the relative value of goods and services, helping them make decisions about what to buy. For producers, prices signal how much of a product to produce or supply. When prices rise, it can signal to producers that there is an opportunity to increase production and profits. Conversely, falling prices may indicate that production needs to be reduced. These price signals help allocate resources efficiently within the economy.

Market Equilibrium

Market equilibrium occurs when the quantity supplied equals the quantity demanded, resulting in a stable price. At this point, there is no excess supply or demand, and the market is considered to be in balance. However, markets are dynamic, and shifts in supply and demand can lead to changes in equilibrium prices. For example, a sudden increase in demand for a popular product can lead to higher prices until supply catches up, while a surplus of goods can lead to price reductions to clear excess inventory.

Consumer Choices

Markets provide consumers with choices, allowing them to select from a variety of goods and services based on their preferences, needs, and budget. The availability of choice in the market encourages competition among producers, leading to innovation, better quality products, and competitive pricing. However, too much choice can also lead to decision fatigue, where consumers feel overwhelmed by the number of options available. Understanding how markets operate can help consumers make informed choices that align with their values and priorities.

The Role of Information

Information is crucial in the functioning of markets. Consumers need accurate information about prices, quality, and availability to make informed decisions, while producers need information about consumer preferences, market trends, and competition to operate effectively. Incomplete or misleading information can lead to market failures, where resources are not allocated efficiently. This is why transparency and access to information are vital for the proper functioning of markets.

Externalities

Markets do not always account for the broader impact of economic activities on society and the environment. Externalities are the positive or negative consequences of market transactions that affect third parties who are not directly involved in the transaction. For example, pollution from a factory is a negative externality that can harm the environment and public health. Governments often intervene in markets to address externalities through regulations, taxes, or subsidies to ensure that the true costs and benefits of economic activities are reflected in market prices.

Market Failures

While markets are generally efficient at allocating resources, they can sometimes fail to produce optimal outcomes. Market failures occur when the market does not allocate resources efficiently or equitably, leading to negative outcomes such as monopolies, income inequality, or environmental degradation. When market failures occur, government intervention may be necessary to correct the inefficiencies and ensure that markets operate in a way that benefits society as a whole.

The Role of Competition

Competition is a driving force in markets, influencing the behaviour of businesses and consumers alike. It plays a critical role in promoting efficiency, innovation, and consumer welfare.

Encouraging Efficiency

In a competitive market, businesses must operate efficiently to survive and thrive. Competition forces companies to minimize costs, optimize production processes, and make the best use of available resources. Efficient businesses can offer lower prices to consumers, which increases their competitiveness in the market. This pressure to improve efficiency benefits consumers by providing them with more affordable options and higher-quality products.

Fostering Innovation

Competition encourages businesses to innovate and differentiate their products and services. In a competitive market, companies must continually seek new ways to attract customers, whether through improved products, better customer service, or innovative business models. This drive for innovation leads to the development of new technologies, products, and services that enhance our quality of life. Without competition, businesses may become complacent, leading to stagnation and a lack of progress.

Consumer Choice and Empowerment

Competition provides consumers with choices, allowing them to select from a variety of products and services that best meet their needs. This choice empowers consumers to make decisions based on factors such as price, quality, and brand reputation. When consumers have the power to choose, businesses are incentivized to improve their offerings to attract and retain customers. In this way, competition ensures that consumers receive the best possible value for their money.

Preventing Monopolies

Competition acts as a check on the power of businesses, preventing any single company from dominating the market. When a company gains too much market power, it can lead to monopolistic practices, such as price gouging, reduced product quality, and a lack of innovation. Governments often regulate markets to ensure that competition remains fair and that monopolistic behaviour is curbed. Antitrust laws and regulations are designed to promote competition and protect consumers from the negative effects of monopolies.

Challenges to Competition

While competition is generally beneficial, it can also present challenges. Intense competition can lead to aggressive business practices, such as price wars, which may harm smaller businesses or reduce overall industry profitability. Additionally, not all markets are equally competitive—some industries, such as utilities or pharmaceuticals, may have high barriers to entry, leading to limited competition. In such cases, regulation may be necessary to ensure that competition serves the public interest.

The Role of Government in Promoting Competition

Governments play a crucial role in promoting and maintaining competition in markets. This can include enforcing antitrust laws, regulating industries with natural monopolies, and encouraging the entry of new competitors into the market. By creating a level playing field, governments help ensure that competition remains healthy and that markets operate efficiently and fairly.

Global Competition

In today's interconnected world, competition is not limited to local or national markets—businesses must also compete on a global scale. Global competition brings both opportunities and challenges. It allows businesses to access new markets and tap into global supply chains, but it also exposes them to competition from foreign companies. To remain competitive, businesses must adapt to global market conditions, innovate continuously, and maintain high standards of quality and efficiency.

In today's globalized economy, companies must navigate the challenges and opportunities of international competition. This often involves adapting to different regulatory environments, consumer preferences, and cultural norms. Global competition can lead to innovation and lower prices as companies strive to gain a competitive edge. However, it can also result in job displacement and wage pressures in industries where competition from lower-cost producers is intense. For consumers, global competition can mean access to a wider variety of goods and services, often at lower prices. However, it also requires consumers to be aware of the origins of products and the implications of their purchasing choices on global supply chains and labour practices.

Ethical Considerations

While competition drives innovation and efficiency, it's also important to consider the ethical implications of competitive practices. Businesses must balance the pursuit of profit with the need to act responsibly, considering the impact of their actions on employees, consumers, and the environment. Ethical competition involves fair practices, transparency, and a commitment to social responsibility. Companies that prioritize ethical behaviour not only build trust with consumers but also contribute positively to the broader community.

Consumer Empowerment in a Competitive Market

In a competitive market, consumers hold significant power. Their choices and preferences can shape market trends, influence product development, and even determine the success or failure of businesses. As consumers become more informed and connected, they are increasingly demanding higher standards of quality, sustainability, and ethical conduct from the companies they support. This shift is leading businesses to adopt more consumer-centric approaches, focusing on creating value beyond just the price point.

Conclusion

Markets, in all their forms, are the beating heart of the economy. From local exchanges to global networks, they influence nearly every aspect of our daily lives, shaping the availability of goods and services, determining prices, and fostering innovation. Understanding how markets operate helps us make more informed decisions as consumers, workers, and citizens.

The power of markets lies not only in their ability to facilitate trade and economic growth but also in their capacity to drive competition and innovation. However, this power must be balanced with ethical considerations and a commitment to social responsibility to ensure that markets serve the broader interests of society.

As we navigate the complexities of modern markets, it's crucial to recognize the role that each of us plays in this dynamic system. By making informed choices, supporting ethical businesses, and advocating for fair competition, we contribute to the creation of markets that are not only efficient and innovative but also just and sustainable.

This understanding of markets and competition is fundamental as we continue to explore the ways in which economics shapes our daily lives. In the chapters that follow, we will delve deeper into specific economic principles and their practical applications, helping you to better navigate the economic landscape and make decisions that enhance your financial well-being and overall quality of life.

7.
SUPPLY AND DEMAND

Supply and demand are the foundational concepts in economics that govern the functioning of markets. These principles explain how prices are determined in a free market, how resources are allocated, and how businesses and consumers make decisions. Understanding supply and demand allows us to make sense of price fluctuations, shortages, surpluses, and the broader economic forces at play in our daily lives.

The Law of Supply and Demand

Understanding Supply and Demand: At its core, the law of supply and demand describes how the quantity of a good or service that is available (supply) and the desire of buyers for it (demand) interact to determine its price. When demand for a product increases and supply remains unchanged, the higher demand leads to a higher equilibrium price. Conversely, if supply increases while demand remains the same, the equilibrium price will fall.

Supply: Supply refers to the various quantities of a product or service that producers are willing and able to sell at different prices. The relationship between price and the quantity supplied is typically direct; as prices increase, suppliers are motivated to produce more to maximize profit. This relationship is depicted by the supply curve, which slopes upwards, as shown below in Diagram 1.

Diagram 1

Demand: Demand, on the other hand, refers to the various quantities of a product or service that consumers are willing and able to purchase at various prices. Generally, the relationship between price and the quantity demanded is inverse; as prices decrease, consumers are more likely to buy more of the product. The demand curve, therefore, slopes downwards, as shown in Diagram 2 below.

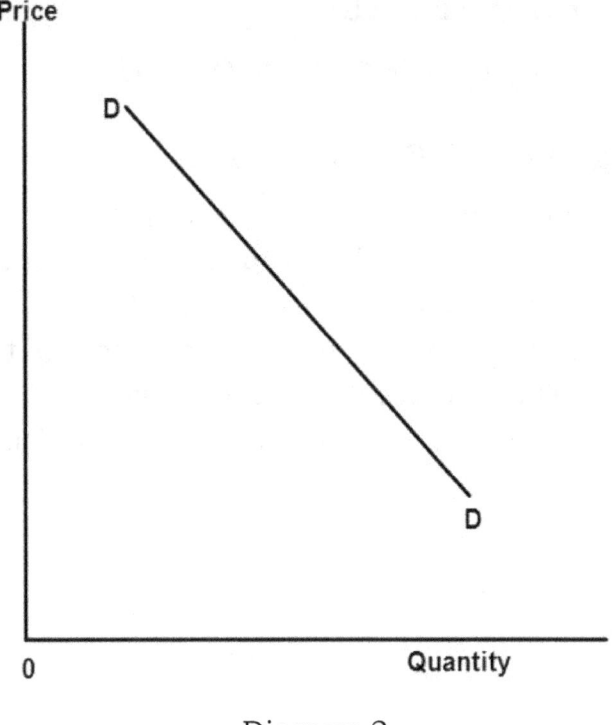

Diagram 2

The Law in Action

The law of supply and demand is observable in many everyday scenarios. For instance, during a heatwave, the demand for air conditioners typically rises. If manufacturers can't increase production quickly enough, the higher demand will lead to higher prices. Conversely, after the holiday season, when demand for certain goods like holiday decorations drops, prices often fall as retailers try to clear excess inventory.

Market Equilibrium: Where Supply Meets Demand

Defining Market Equilibrium

Market equilibrium occurs when the quantity of a good or service supplied equals the quantity demanded at a particular price level. At this point, the market is in balance, and there is no inherent pressure for the price to change. The equilibrium price is where the supply and demand curves intersect as shown in Diagram 3 below.

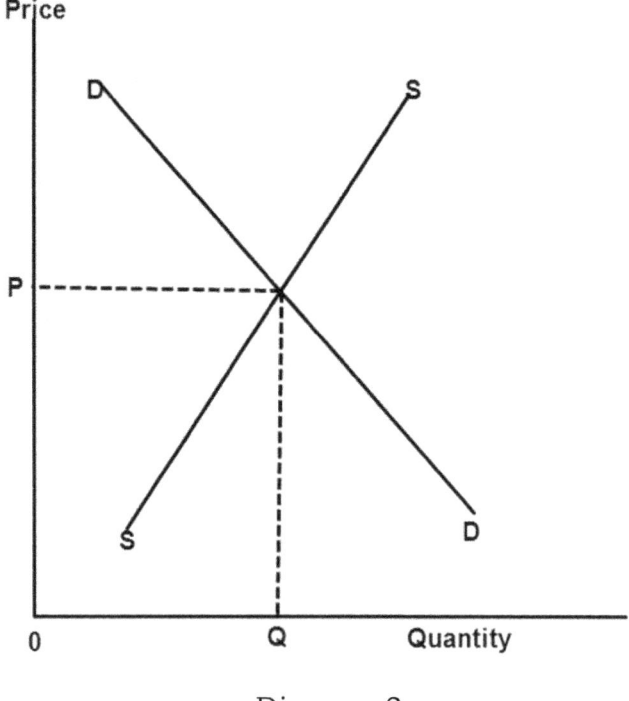

Diagram 3

The equilibrium price is P and the equilibrium quantity is Q.

Reaching Equilibrium

In a competitive market, prices naturally move toward equilibrium. If the market price is above the equilibrium level, there is a surplus—more goods are available than consumers want to buy at that price. To clear the surplus, sellers may reduce prices, which increases the quantity demanded and decreases the quantity supplied until equilibrium is reached. Conversely, if the price is below equilibrium, a shortage occurs—the quantity demanded exceeds the quantity supplied. In response, prices tend to rise, which reduces the quantity demanded and increases the quantity supplied until the market reaches equilibrium.

Shifts in Supply and Demand

Market equilibrium can be disrupted by shifts in supply and demand. For example, a technological breakthrough that lowers production costs can increase supply, shifting the supply curve to the right and lowering the equilibrium price as shown in Diagram 4 below. Alternatively, a sudden increase in consumer preferences for a product can increase demand, shifting the demand curve to the right and raising the equilibrium price as shown in Diagram 5 below.

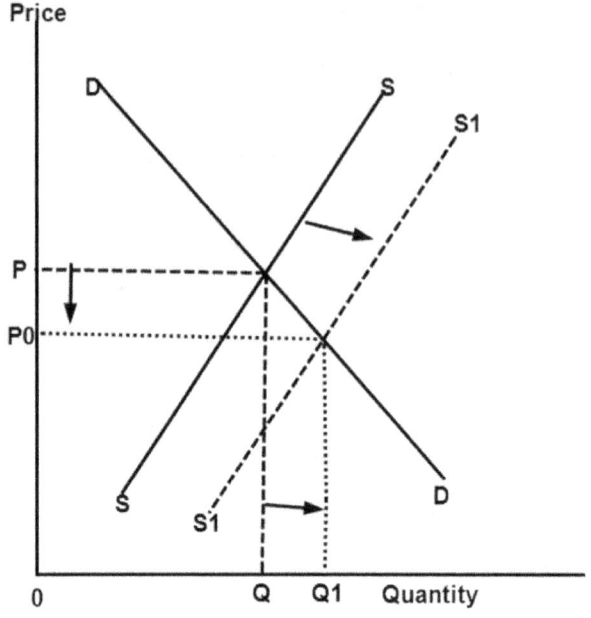

Diagram 4

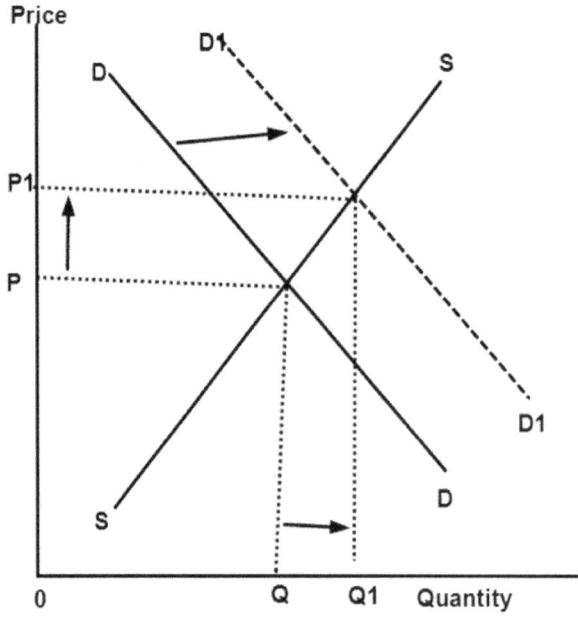

Diagram 5

Real-World Examples:

Consider the housing market. If a city experiences a population boom, demand for housing increases, driving up prices. However, if new construction increases the supply of homes, the market may eventually reach a new equilibrium where prices stabilize. Similarly, in the agricultural market, a bad harvest can reduce the supply of a crop like wheat, leading to higher prices until the next harvest restores supply and brings prices back to equilibrium.

How Supply and Demand Affect Prices

Price Determination

Supply and demand are the key determinants of prices in a market economy. When the quantity demanded of a good or service exceeds the quantity supplied, price rises, signaling producers to increase production. Conversely, when the quantity supplied exceeds the quantity demanded, the price falls, signaling producers to decrease production.

Elasticity of Supply and Demand

The sensitivity of quantity supplied and quantity demanded to changes in price is known as elasticity. If a small change in price leads to a relatively large change in the quantity demanded or supplied, the demand for or supply of the good or service is considered elastic. For example, luxury goods often have elastic demand because consumers can easily forego them if prices rise. In contrast, necessities like food and fuel typically have inelastic demand; even if prices rise, consumers still need to buy them, so the quantity demanded changes little.

Price Controls and Their Effects

Governments sometimes intervene in markets by imposing price controls, such as price ceilings (maximum prices) or price floors (minimum prices). While these controls can protect consumers and producers in the short term, they can also lead to unintended consequences. For example, a price ceiling on rent may make housing more affordable, but it can also lead to a shortage of available rental properties as landlords are less incentivized to rent out or maintain their properties.

Case Studies in Supply and Demand

Oil Prices: The global oil market is a classic example of supply and demand dynamics. Events that disrupt supply, such as geopolitical conflicts or natural disasters, can lead to sharp increases in oil prices. Conversely, technological advances in oil extraction can increase supply and lower prices. Similarly, changes in global demand, such as shifts toward renewable energy, can impact oil prices.

Technology Products: The release of a new smartphone often illustrates supply and demand principles. Initial high demand can lead to shortages and high prices. Over time, as supply increases and demand stabilizes, prices often decrease. Additionally, the introduction of newer models can shift demand away from older versions, leading to price reductions for those models.

Conclusion

The principles of supply and demand are fundamental to understanding how markets function. These forces determine the prices of goods and services, allocate resources and influence economic behaviour. By understanding supply and demand, individuals can make more informed decisions as consumers, workers, and investors. Whether you are buying groceries, negotiating a salary, or investing in the stock market, the concepts of supply and demand are at play, shaping the economic landscape in which we all live and operate.

In the following chapters, we will explore more economic principles and how they impact everyday life, helping you navigate the complexities of the economy with greater confidence and understanding.

8.
THE ECONOMICS OF TIME MANAGEMENT

Time is one of the most valuable resources we possess, yet it is often overlooked in economic discussions. Unlike money, time cannot be saved or stored; once it is spent, it is gone forever. Understanding the economics of time management is crucial for maximizing productivity, achieving personal and professional goals, and maintaining a balanced life. In this chapter, we will explore how to value time as an economic resource, implement effective time management strategies, and find the right balance between work, leisure, and family time.

Valuing Time as an Economic Resource

Understanding Time as a Scarce Resource

In economics, scarcity refers to the limited nature of resources, and time is perhaps the most limited of all. We each have 24 hours in a day, and how we allocate those hours can significantly impact our overall well-being and success. Valuing time means recognizing its importance in decision-making and treating it as a finite resource that must be managed wisely.

The Opportunity Cost of Time

The concept of opportunity cost is central to understanding the value of time. Every choice we make involves a trade-off, where choosing one activity means forgoing another. For example, spending an extra hour at work might increase your income, but it comes at the cost of time spent with family or pursuing hobbies. Recognizing these trade-offs helps us make more informed decisions about how to use our time.

Time vs. Money: The Trade-Off

Many people struggle with the trade-off between time and money. For instance, you might choose to work longer hours to earn more money, but this can lead to burnout and reduced quality of life. Alternatively, you might opt for a job with fewer hours and less pay but gain more time for personal pursuits. Understanding this trade-off is key to finding a balance that aligns with your values and long-term goals.

Time Management Strategies for Maximizing Productivity

Setting Priorities

Effective time management begins with setting clear priorities. Not all tasks are of equal importance, and learning to distinguish between what is urgent and what is important can help you focus on activities that truly matter. Techniques like the Eisenhower Matrix, which categorizes tasks based on urgency and importance, can be invaluable in this process.

The Power of Planning

Planning is a critical component of time management. By setting specific goals and creating a structured plan to achieve them, you can make better use of your time. Daily to-do lists, weekly planners, and long-term goal-setting are tools that can help you stay organized and ensure that your time is spent on activities that contribute to your personal and professional growth.

Avoiding Time Wasters

Identifying and eliminating time-wasting activities is essential for maximizing productivity. Common time wasters include excessive social media use, unnecessary meetings, and procrastination. By becoming aware of these habits and actively working to minimize them, you can free up time for more productive and fulfilling activities. Here is a list of 10 time wasters that you should avoid:

    Meetings

    Multitasking

    Procrastination

    Disorganization

    Perfectionism

    Clutter

    Lack of prioritization

    Talking too long on the phone

    Focusing on smaller, less important tasks

    Incessantly preparing and not taking action

The Role of Technology in Time Management

Technology can be both a boon and a bane when it comes to time management. On the one hand, tools like productivity apps, calendar management software, and automation can help you manage your time more efficiently. On the other hand, constant notifications, emails, and digital distractions can derail your focus. Learning to use technology mindfully is crucial for staying on track.

Balancing Work, Leisure, and Family Time

The Importance of Work-Life Balance

Achieving a balance between work, leisure, and family time is essential for long-term happiness and well-being. Overemphasizing work can lead to stress, burnout, and strained relationships while neglecting work can impact financial stability and career growth. Striking the right balance requires intentionality and a commitment to prioritizing all aspects of life.

Creating Boundaries Between Work and Personal Life

One of the biggest challenges in modern life is creating clear boundaries between work and personal time, especially with the rise of remote work and constant connectivity. Setting boundaries, such as designated work hours, unplugging from technology during family time, and taking regular breaks, can help ensure that each area of your life receives the attention it deserves.

The Value of Leisure and Rest

Leisure and rest are often undervalued in our productivity-focused society, but they are critical for maintaining mental and physical health. Taking time to relax, pursue hobbies, and enjoy the company of loved ones can rejuvenate your mind and body, making you more effective in all areas of life. Recognizing the economic value of rest—such as its impact on productivity and creativity—can help you prioritize it.

Incorporating Family Time into Daily Life

Family time is an investment in relationships that yields long-term benefits. Whether it's sharing meals, engaging in activities together, or simply spending quality time with loved ones, these moments contribute to stronger family bonds and a more fulfilling life. Planning and scheduling family time, just as you would work commitments, ensures that it remains a priority.

Conclusion

The economics of time management is about more than just squeezing the most productivity out of every day; it's about making intentional choices that align with your values, goals, and well-being. By understanding the value of time, implementing effective time management strategies, and finding a balance between work, leisure, and family life, you can create a more fulfilling and purpose-driven life. Time is a resource that once spent, cannot be regained, so managing it wisely is essential for achieving lasting success and happiness.

9.
GOVERNMENT AND THE ECONOMY

The relationship between government and the economy is complex and multifaceted, impacting nearly every aspect of our daily lives. From the taxes we pay to the regulations that shape our industries, government policies play a crucial role in determining the economic landscape. This chapter delves into the ways in which government influences the economy, focusing on the essential areas of taxation, public services, regulation, and the delicate balance between free markets and government intervention.

Taxes and Public Services

The Role of Taxes in Society

Taxes are the primary means by which governments fund public services and infrastructure. Whether it's roads, schools, healthcare, or defense, the services that we often take for granted are largely financed by tax revenues. Understanding the different types of taxes—such as income, property, sales, and corporate taxes—and how they are levied is crucial for grasping their impact on both individual households and the broader economy.

The Benefits of Public Services

Public services, funded by taxes, are essential for the functioning of society. They provide a safety net for the vulnerable, promote economic stability, and contribute to the overall quality of life. For instance, public education helps to ensure a more skilled workforce, while public healthcare provides essential medical services that might be unaffordable otherwise. These services are investments in the long-term well-being of society, with broad economic implications.

The Tax Burden and Its Distribution

The concept of the tax burden refers to how much tax individuals and businesses are required to pay and how this burden is distributed across different income groups. Progressive tax systems, where higher earners pay a larger percentage of their income in taxes, aim to reduce income inequality and fund social programs. Conversely, regressive taxes, which take a larger percentage of income from lower earners, can exacerbate inequality. Understanding these dynamics is essential for informed discussions about tax policy.

The Impact of Taxes on Economic Behaviour:

Taxes influence economic behaviour in significant ways. High taxes on income might discourage work or investment, while tax incentives can encourage activities like home ownership, education, and energy efficiency. The design of a tax system must consider these behavioural impacts to achieve the desired economic outcomes without unintended consequences.

Government Regulation and Its Impact

The Purpose of Government Regulation

Government regulation is designed to protect consumers, workers, and the environment, as well as to ensure fair competition in the marketplace. Regulations can take many forms, including safety standards, environmental protections, labour laws, and antitrust laws. These regulations help prevent abuses, reduce risks, and create a level playing field for businesses.

The Benefits of Regulation

Regulation provides essential safeguards in areas where free markets might fail. For example, environmental regulations help to reduce pollution and protect public health, while financial regulations aim to prevent economic crises by ensuring the stability of financial institutions. Worker protections, such as minimum wage laws and safety standards, ensure that employees are treated fairly and work in safe conditions.

The Costs of Regulation

While regulation offers significant benefits, it also imposes costs on businesses and the economy. Compliance with regulations can be expensive and time-consuming, potentially stifling innovation or reducing profitability. Small businesses, in particular, may struggle to meet regulatory requirements, leading to barriers to entry in certain industries. The challenge lies in finding a balance where regulations protect public interests without unduly burdening businesses.

The Debate Over Deregulation

Deregulation—the reduction or elimination of government regulations—is often advocated as a means of promoting economic growth and reducing costs. Proponents argue that less regulation can lead to increased efficiency, lower prices, and greater innovation. However, critics warn that deregulation can lead to negative consequences, such as reduced consumer protections, environmental degradation, and financial instability. The debate over deregulation is a central issue in economic policy.

The Balance Between Free Markets and Government Intervention

The Philosophy of Free Markets

Free markets operate on the principle that individuals and businesses, guided by self-interest, can make better economic decisions than a centralized authority. In a free market, prices are determined by supply and demand, and competition drives innovation and efficiency. Proponents of free markets argue that minimal government intervention allows for more efficient allocation of resources and greater economic freedom.

The Need for Government Intervention

While free markets have many advantages, they are not without flaws. Market failures, such as monopolies, externalities (like pollution), and information asymmetry, can lead to inefficient outcomes and harm public welfare. Government intervention is often necessary to correct these failures, ensure fair competition, and protect public interests. Examples of intervention include antitrust laws, subsidies for renewable energy, and social welfare programs.

Striking the Right Balance

The challenge for policymakers is to strike the right balance between free markets and government intervention. Too much intervention can stifle economic freedom and lead to inefficiencies, while too little can result in market failures and social inequalities. The ideal balance varies depending on the specific economic context, societal values, and the goals of public policy.

Case Studies in Balancing Intervention

Looking at real-world examples can provide insight into how different countries balance free markets and government intervention. For instance, the Nordic countries are known for their combination of free-market capitalism and extensive welfare states, while the United States has a more market-oriented approach with less direct government intervention. These case studies highlight the diversity of approaches and the outcomes they produce.

Conclusion

Government plays a pivotal role in shaping the economy through taxation, regulation, and intervention. Understanding these dynamics is essential for anyone interested in economics, as they affect every aspect of daily life—from the services we rely on to the prices we pay and the opportunities available in the marketplace.

By exploring the intricate relationship between government and the economy, we gain a deeper appreciation of the balance that must be maintained to promote both economic efficiency and social welfare.

10.
INVESTING AND GROWING WEALTH

Investing is one of the most effective ways to build wealth over time. While earning and saving money are important, investing allows you to grow your wealth by putting your money to work. Understanding the principles of investing, the various types of investment vehicles, and the strategies for managing risk is crucial for anyone looking to secure his or her financial future. This chapter explores the basics of investing, the balance between risk and reward, and the importance of planning for retirement.

Basics of Investing: Stocks, Bonds, and Real Estate

Understanding Stocks

Stocks represent ownership in a company, and investing in stocks allows you to become a part-owner of that business. As a shareholder, you may benefit from the company's growth through price appreciation and dividends. Stocks are generally considered to be higher-risk investments because their value can fluctuate significantly, but they also offer the potential for high returns over the long term. Understanding how to evaluate stocks and diversify your portfolio is key to successful investing.

The Role of Bonds in an Investment Portfolio

Bonds are debt instruments issued by governments or corporations to raise money. When you purchase a bond, you are essentially lending money to the issuer in exchange for regular interest payments and the return of the bond's face value at maturity. Bonds are typically considered lower-risk investments compared to stocks, making them a good option for those looking for more stable returns. However, the potential for growth is usually lower, and understanding the relationship between interest rates and bond prices is crucial for bond investors.

Investing in Real Estate

Real estate is another popular investment vehicle, offering the potential for both income and capital appreciation. Whether through direct ownership of property or through real estate investment trusts (REITs), real estate can provide a steady income stream and a hedge against inflation. However, it also requires significant capital and comes with risks such as market volatility and property management challenges. Knowing the local real estate market, the costs associated with property ownership, and the long-term prospects of real estate investments are important factors to consider.

Diversification Across Asset Classes

Diversification involves spreading your investments across different asset classes—such as stocks, bonds, and real estate—to reduce risk. By holding a diversified portfolio, you can protect yourself from significant losses if one particular investment performs poorly. Diversification is a fundamental principle of investing, helping to stabilize returns and manage risk over time.

The Risk-Reward Trade-off

Understanding Risk and Reward

In investing, risk and reward are inherently linked—the higher the potential return, the higher the risk. Understanding this tradeoff is crucial for making informed investment decisions. High-risk investments, like stocks and certain real estate ventures, can offer substantial returns, but they also come with the possibility of significant losses. On the other hand, low-risk investments, such as bonds or savings accounts, offer more stable returns but with less potential for growth.

Risk Tolerance and Investment Goals

Your risk tolerance—how much risk you are willing to take—should align with your investment goals and time horizon. For example, younger investors with a long-term horizon might afford to take on more risk, as they have more time to recover from potential losses. Conversely, those nearing retirement might prefer safer investments to preserve their capital. It's important to assess your risk tolerance and create an investment strategy that aligns with your financial goals.

The Importance of Time Horizon

The time horizon—the length of time you expect to hold an investment before needing to access the funds—also plays a significant role in the risk-reward tradeoff. Investments in volatile assets, like stocks, may perform well over the long term, but they can be risky in the short term. Understanding your time horizon helps you choose the right mix of investments and manage risk effectively.

Strategies for Managing Investment Risk

There are several strategies to manage risk in your investment portfolio, including diversification, asset allocation, and regular portfolio reviews. Diversification, as discussed earlier, spreads risk across different asset classes. Asset allocation involves adjusting the mix of assets in your portfolio based on your risk tolerance, investment goals, and market conditions. Regularly reviewing and rebalancing your portfolio ensures that it remains aligned with your financial objectives and risk tolerance.

Planning for Retirement

The Importance of Early Planning

Planning for retirement is one of the most important financial goals, and starting early gives you a significant advantage. The power of compounding—where your investment earnings generate their own earnings—means that even small contributions made early on can grow substantially over time. Understanding the different retirement savings vehicles, such as 401(k)s,

IRAs, and pensions, is essential for building a retirement nest egg.

Choosing the Right Retirement Accounts

Retirement accounts, such as 401(k)s and IRAs, in the United States, and RSPS in Canada, offer tax advantages that can help your savings grow more efficiently. A 401(k) allows you to contribute pre-tax income, reducing your taxable income, while an IRA offers the choice between traditional (tax-deferred) and Roth (tax-free growth) options. Knowing the benefits and limitations of each account type helps you choose the right one based on your income, tax situation, and retirement goals.

Determining How Much to Save

A key question in retirement planning is how much you need to save to maintain your desired lifestyle in retirement. This depends on factors like your expected expenses, life expectancy, and inflation. Financial planners often recommend saving enough to replace 70% to 80% of your pre-retirement income. Regularly reviewing and adjusting your savings rate, as well as factoring in other sources of income like Social Security or pensions, ensures that you stay on track.

The Role of Investments in Retirement Planning

Investments play a crucial role in growing your retirement savings. As you approach retirement, your investment strategy may shift from growth-oriented to income-oriented, focusing more on preserving capital and generating a steady income. Balancing growth and security in your investment portfolio helps ensure that your savings last throughout your retirement years.

Conclusion

Investing and growing wealth is a journey that requires knowledge, patience, and a well-thought-out strategy. By understanding the basics of investing, the risk-reward tradeoff, and the importance of planning for retirement, you can make informed decisions that will help you achieve your financial goals. Whether you're just starting or are well on your way, the principles outlined in this chapter provide a solid foundation for building and preserving wealth over the long term.

11.
ECONOMIC CYCLES AND YOU

Understanding Booms and Busts

Economic cycles, often referred to as booms and busts, are the natural fluctuations in economic activity that occur over time. These cycles are characterized by periods of expansion, known as booms, followed by periods of contraction, known as busts. During a boom, the economy experiences rapid growth, increased consumer spending, and higher levels of employment. Businesses thrive, investments increase, and confidence in the market is high. However, booms are often followed by busts—periods of economic downturn where growth slows, unemployment rises, and spending decreases.

Understanding these cycles is crucial for individuals and businesses alike. During booms, it's important not to overextend finances or take on too much debt, as the following bust could make repayment difficult. Conversely, during busts, opportunities for investment and growth often emerge, as prices fall and new market conditions develop. Recognizing the signs of economic cycles can help you make informed decisions that align with the current phase of the economy.

How Economic Cycles Affect Employment and Spending

Economic cycles have a direct impact on employment and consumer spending. During a boom, businesses expand, creating more jobs and higher wages, which in turn increases consumer spending. People feel more confident in their financial stability and are more likely to make large purchases, invest in new ventures, and take financial risks. This increased spending fuels further economic growth, creating a positive feedback loop.

However, during a bust, the opposite occurs. Businesses may downsize or close, leading to job losses and reduced wages. As a result, consumer confidence drops, and people tend to cut back on spending, particularly on non-essential items. This reduction in spending can prolong the economic downturn, as businesses struggle with lower revenues and may be forced to lay off more workers or reduce investments. Understanding the relationship between economic cycles, employment, and spending can help you prepare for the financial implications of both boom and bust periods.

Preparing for Economic Uncertainty

Economic uncertainty is an inevitable part of life, as it's impossible to predict with complete accuracy when a boom or bust will occur. However, there are strategies you can employ to protect yourself and your finances during periods of economic instability. One of the most important steps is to create an emergency fund—a financial safety net that can cover your living expenses for several months in case of job loss or other financial challenges. This fund can provide peace of mind and stability during a downturn.

Another key strategy is to maintain a diversified investment portfolio. By spreading your investments across different asset classes, such as stocks, bonds, and real estate, you can reduce the risk of significant losses during a downturn. Additionally, keeping your skills up to date and continuously improving your employability can help you remain competitive in the job market, even during periods of high unemployment.

Lastly, it's important to stay informed about the economy and to adjust your financial plans as needed. Being proactive and adaptable can help you navigate economic cycles with greater confidence and resilience, ensuring that you are better prepared for both the highs and lows of the economy.

12.
GLOBAL ECONOMICS

The Impact of Global Trade on Daily Life

Global trade is the backbone of modern economies, influencing everything from the availability of products on store shelves to job opportunities in local communities. At its core, global trade is the exchange of goods and services across international borders, and it has been a driving force in economic development for centuries. The interconnectedness of economies around the world means that the decisions made by businesses, governments, and consumers in one country can have a ripple effect across the globe.

One of the most visible impacts of global trade is the diversity of products available to consumers. In many parts of the world, it is possible to purchase tropical fruits, electronics, clothing, and countless other goods that are not produced locally. This variety is a direct result of global supply chains, which involve the production, transportation, and sale of goods across multiple countries. For example, a smartphone might be designed in the United States, assembled in China, and sold in Europe, with components sourced from multiple countries along the way.

However, the benefits of global trade come with challenges. Supply chains can be fragile, and disruptions—such as natural disasters, political instability, or pandemics—can lead to shortages and price increases. The COVID-19 pandemic, for example, exposed vulnerabilities in global supply chains, leading to delays and higher costs for everything from medical supplies to consumer electronics.

Global trade also has a significant impact on employment. While it can create jobs in industries that benefit from export opportunities, it can also lead to job losses in sectors that face competition from cheaper imported goods. This dynamic is often referred to as "offshoring," where companies relocate production to countries with lower labour costs, resulting in job displacement in their home countries. On the flip side, global trade can lead to the creation of new industries and opportunities for innovation, as businesses adapt to the changing economic landscape.

For consumers, understanding global trade is essential for making informed decisions. Being aware of where products come from, how they are made, and the factors that influence their availability and cost can help individuals make more conscious choices. Additionally, staying informed about trade policies and international relations can provide insights into potential economic shifts that may affect household budgets and long-term financial planning.

Currency Exchange and Its Effects

Currency exchange is a fundamental aspect of global economics that affects everyone, whether they realize it or not. At its most basic level, currency exchange involves converting one currency into another, and this process is influenced by various factors, including interest rates, inflation, political stability, and economic performance.

For travelers, currency exchange rates determine how far their money will go when visiting another country. A favourable exchange rate means that travelers can get more foreign currency for their money, making their trip more affordable. Conversely, an unfavourable exchange rate can make travel more expensive and limit purchasing power.

However, the impact of currency exchange extends far beyond travel. Businesses that engage in international trade must constantly monitor exchange rates, as fluctuations can significantly affect their profitability. For example, a company that exports goods to another country will earn revenue in the foreign currency. If the value of that currency falls relative to the company's home currency, the revenue will be worth less when converted back, potentially leading to losses. To manage this risk, businesses often engage in hedging strategies, such as forward contracts, to lock in exchange rates and protect against adverse movements.

For consumers, currency exchange rates influence the prices of imported goods. When the domestic currency is strong, imports become cheaper, as it takes fewer units of the domestic currency to buy foreign goods. This can lead to lower prices for a wide range of products, from electronics to clothing. Conversely, a weak domestic currency can make imports more expensive, leading to higher prices for consumers.

Currency fluctuations can also impact investments. Many investors hold assets in foreign currencies, such as stocks, bonds, or real estate. Changes in exchange rates can affect the value of these investments, adding an additional layer of complexity to financial planning. For example, U.S. investors who hold European stocks may see the value of their portfolio rise or fall depending on the exchange rate between the euro and the dollar, even if the underlying value of the stocks remains unchanged.

Understanding currency exchange is crucial for making informed financial decisions, whether traveling, investing, or purchasing goods from international markets. By staying informed about global economic conditions and monitoring exchange rates, individuals can better manage their financial resources and protect themselves from the risks associated with currency fluctuations.

How Global Events Influence Local Economies

In today's interconnected world, global events can have profound and immediate effects on local economies. Whether it's a natural disaster, political upheaval, or a global health crisis, events in one part of the world can quickly influence economic conditions elsewhere, highlighting the interconnected nature of modern economies.

Natural disasters, such as hurricanes, earthquakes, or tsunamis, can disrupt global supply chains, leading to shortages and price increases for essential goods. For example, a hurricane in the Gulf of Mexico can disrupt oil production, leading to higher fuel prices worldwide. Similarly, an earthquake in Japan, a major producer of electronic components, can create shortages in the global electronics market, driving up prices for consumers around the world.

Political events, such as elections, trade wars, or international sanctions, can also have significant economic impacts. The uncertainty surrounding political events can lead to volatility in financial markets, affecting stock prices, exchange rates, and interest rates. For example, the uncertainty surrounding Brexit, the United Kingdom's decision to leave the European Union, led to fluctuations in the value of the British pound and created uncertainty for businesses and consumers in both the UK and the EU.

Trade wars, in particular, can have widespread effects on global and local economies. When countries impose tariffs or other trade barriers on each other's goods, it can lead to higher prices for consumers, reduced exports for businesses, and disruptions in supply chains. For example, the trade war between the United States and China led to higher prices for a range of goods, from electronics to agricultural products, affecting both producers and consumers in both countries.

Global health crises, such as the COVID-19 pandemic, can have far-reaching economic impacts. The pandemic led to widespread lockdowns, disrupting businesses, reducing consumer spending, and leading to mass unemployment. Governments around the world responded with unprecedented fiscal and monetary measures, including stimulus packages and interest rate cuts, to stabilize their economies. The long-term economic effects of the pandemic are still unfolding, but it has underscored the importance of resilience and preparedness in the face of global challenges.

For individuals, understanding the potential impact of global events on local economies is essential for navigating economic uncertainty. By staying informed about global developments and their potential economic implications, individuals can make better decisions about spending, saving, and investing. Additionally, understanding the interconnectedness of global and local economies can help individuals appreciate the broader context in which their economic lives are situated.

Conclusion

Global economics may seem complex and distant, but it has a direct impact on our everyday lives. From the products we buy to the value of our investments, the global economy shapes the choices we make and the opportunities available to us. By understanding the basics of global trade, currency exchange, and the impact of global events, individuals can better navigate the complexities of the modern economy.

As the world becomes increasingly interconnected, the importance of understanding global economics will only grow. Whether you are a consumer, a worker, an investor, or a business owner, staying informed about global economic trends and developments is essential for making informed decisions and achieving financial success. By recognizing the impact of global economics on your daily life, you can better prepare for the future and make choices that enhance your financial well-being.

13.
CONSUMER BEHAVIOUR AND DECISION-MAKING

The Psychology Behind Spending Choices

Consumer behaviour is deeply rooted in psychology. A complex interplay of emotions, cognitive biases, social influences, and personal habits often influences our spending choices. Understanding the psychological mechanisms behind these choices can provide valuable insights into why we make the decisions we do when it comes to spending money.

Emotional Spending

Emotions play a significant role in consumer behaviour. For example, people often engage in "retail therapy," purchasing items to improve their mood or cope with stress. This type of emotional spending can provide temporary relief but may lead to financial strain if done excessively. Conversely, feelings of guilt or fear can lead to more cautious spending, as individuals may avoid making purchases that they perceive as frivolous or unnecessary.

Impulse Buying

Impulse buying is another common behaviour driven by psychological factors. It occurs when a consumer makes an unplanned purchase, often triggered by an emotional reaction to a product or its presentation. Retailers take advantage of this by strategically placing items near checkout counters or creating a sense of urgency with limited-time offers. Understanding the triggers for impulse buying can help consumers develop strategies to resist these urges and make more deliberate purchasing decisions.

Cognitive Dissonance

Cognitive dissonance refers to the mental discomfort that occurs when a person holds two conflicting beliefs or attitudes, particularly after making a purchase. For example, after buying some expensive items, consumers might experience dissonance if they start doubting the necessity or value of the purchases. To resolve this discomfort, they may seek out information that justifies the purchase or avoid information that contradicts their decision. This phenomenon explains why consumers often stick to their buying decisions, even when they have doubts.

The Role of Social Proof

Social proof is the psychological concept that individuals tend to follow the actions and opinions of others, particularly when they are uncertain about what to do. This can be seen in consumer behavior when people are influenced by reviews, testimonials, and the purchasing habits of their peers. Marketers capitalize on this by highlighting popular products or using celebrity endorsements to create a sense of trust and desirability.

Loss Aversion

Loss aversion is the tendency for people to prefer avoiding losses over acquiring equivalent gains. This concept plays a significant role in consumer decision-making, as individuals are often more motivated by the fear of missing out (FOMO) or losing something they value than by the potential benefits of a purchase. For example, a consumer might be more inclined to buy a product if he or she perceives that a discount or special offer is about to expire.

Anchoring Effect

The anchoring effect occurs when people rely too heavily on the first piece of information they receive when making a decision. In the context of consumer behaviour, this could mean that a shopper perceives a sale price as a great deal because he or she is anchored to the original, higher price, even if the sale price is still higher than the item's true value. Retailers use anchoring to their advantage by presenting high "original" prices next to discounted ones, making the latter seem like a better deal.

Understanding these psychological factors can help consumers recognize when they might be making decisions based on emotion rather than logic. By being aware of these influences, individuals can take steps to make more informed and rational purchasing choices, ultimately leading to better financial outcomes.

Factors That Influence Consumer Decisions

Several factors influence consumer decisions, ranging from personal preferences to broader economic conditions. Understanding these factors can help consumers make more informed choices and allow businesses to better cater to their target audiences.

Cultural and Social Influences

Culture plays a significant role in shaping consumer behaviour. Cultural values, traditions, and social norms influence what people buy, how they use products, and the importance they place on certain goods and services. For instance, in some cultures, luxury items may be seen as status symbols, leading to higher demand for premium brands. Social influences, such as family, friends, and social networks, also impact consumer decisions. People often seek approval from their social circles, leading them to purchase products that align with the expectations and preferences of their peers.

Economic Factors

The overall economic environment, including factors such as income levels, employment rates, inflation, and interest rates, significantly affects consumer behaviour. During periods of economic growth, consumers tend to have more disposable income and are more likely to make discretionary purchases. Conversely, during economic downturns, consumers may cut back on spending, prioritize essential goods, and become more price-sensitive. Understanding the economic context can help consumers make decisions that align with their financial situation.

Personal Preferences and Lifestyles

Individual preferences and lifestyles play a critical role in shaping consumer behaviour. These preferences are often influenced by factors such as age, gender, education, and life stage. For example, a young professional might prioritize convenience and technology in his or her purchasing decisions, while a retiree might focus more on health and leisure. Understanding one's personal preferences can help consumers make choices that enhance their quality of life and align with their values.

Psychological Needs and Motivations

Maslow's hierarchy of needs provides a useful framework for understanding how psychological needs influence consumer behaviour. According to this theory, individuals are motivated to fulfill their basic physiological needs (such as food and shelter) before seeking to satisfy higher-level needs such as safety, love, esteem, and self-actualization. This hierarchy influences purchasing decisions, as consumers seek products that meet their current needs and aspirations. For instance, a consumer may prioritize buying healthy food to satisfy his or her physiological needs, but once that need is met, he or she may focus on purchasing items that enhance his or her self-esteem or personal growth.

Technological Advances

Technology has dramatically changed consumer behaviour in recent years. The rise of e-commerce, mobile shopping, and social media has transformed how people research products, make purchases, and interact with brands. Technology also enables consumers to access a wealth of information, including reviews, price comparisons, and product specifications, empowering them to make more informed decisions. Additionally, technology-driven innovations such as personalized recommendations and targeted advertising can influence consumer behaviour by presenting products that align with individual preferences and past purchasing behaviour.

Environmental and Ethical Considerations

Increasingly, consumers are considering environmental and ethical factors in their purchasing decisions. Concerns about sustainability, climate change, and fair labour practices have led many consumers to seek out eco-friendly, ethically produced, and socially responsible products. This shift in consumer behaviour is driving demand for products that minimize environmental impact and support ethical business practices. Companies that align with these values are often rewarded with customer loyalty and positive brand perception.

By understanding the various factors that influence consumer decisions, individuals can become more conscious of the external and internal forces shaping their behaviour. This awareness can lead to more intentional and thoughtful purchasing decisions, ultimately benefiting both consumers and society as a whole.

The Impact of Advertising on Buying Habits

Advertising is a powerful tool that significantly influences consumer behaviour. Through various media channels, advertisers use persuasive techniques to capture attention, create desire, and drive purchasing decisions. Understanding the impact of advertising can help consumers make more informed choices and recognize when marketing tactics are influencing them.

Creating Awareness and Desire

One of the primary goals of advertising is to create awareness of a product or service. Advertisers use compelling visuals, catchy slogans, and emotional appeals to capture consumers' attention and make their products stand out in a crowded marketplace. By repeatedly exposing consumers to a brand or product, advertisers aim to build familiarity and trust, ultimately leading to increased desire and likelihood of purchase.

Branding and Identity

Branding is a key aspect of advertising that shapes how consumers perceive a product or company. Effective branding goes beyond the product itself, creating an identity that resonates with consumers on an emotional level. For example, a brand may position itself as a symbol of luxury, innovation, or social responsibility, appealing to consumers' values and aspirations. This branding can influence consumer decisions by creating a sense of loyalty and preference for a particular brand over others, even when competing products offer similar features or benefits.

Emotional Appeals

Advertisers often use emotional appeals to connect with consumers on a deeper level. By tapping into emotions such as happiness, fear, nostalgia, or empathy, advertisers can create a strong emotional bond between the consumer and the product. For instance, a commercial that shows a family enjoying a meal together may evoke feelings of warmth and togetherness, leading consumers to associate those positive emotions with the advertised food product. Emotional appeals can be especially effective in driving impulse purchases, as they bypass rational decision-making processes and trigger immediate responses.

Social Proof and Testimonials

Social proof is a powerful psychological phenomenon that advertisers leverage to influence consumer behaviour. By showcasing testimonials, reviews, or endorsements from satisfied customers or celebrities, advertisers create a sense of credibility and trust. Consumers are more likely to purchase a product if they believe that others have had positive experiences with it. This effect is amplified by the use of influencers on social media, who often promote products to their followers, creating a sense of social validation and desirability.

Scarcity and Urgency

Advertisers often create a sense of scarcity and urgency to encourage consumers to make quick purchasing decisions. Limited-time offers, flash sales, and phrases like "while supplies last" are common tactics used to create the perception that a product is in high demand and may not be available for long. This strategy taps into consumers' fear of missing out (FOMO) and can lead to impulse buying. By understanding this tactic, consumers can resist the pressure to make hasty decisions and take the time to evaluate whether a purchase is truly necessary.

Subliminal Messaging

While overt advertising is easy to recognize, subliminal messaging operates below the threshold of conscious awareness. Subliminal advertising involves embedding subtle cues or messages within ads that can influence consumers' attitudes and behaviours without their realizing it. These cues can take the form of faint images, background sounds, or quick flashes of text that are not consciously noticed but can affect a consumer's subconscious mind. Although the effectiveness of subliminal advertising is still debated, it highlights how deeply advertisers may go to influence purchasing decisions.

Persuasion Techniques

Advertising is fundamentally about persuasion. Advertisers use various persuasive techniques to convince consumers that their product is the best choice. These techniques can include the use of authority (e.g., endorsements by experts or celebrities), appealing to consumers' need for social acceptance (e.g., showing popular individuals using the product), or creating a problem that the product conveniently solves (e.g., "Are you tired of…? This product is the answer!").

Another common persuasive technique is the use of storytelling in ads. Advertisers can make their products more relatable and memorable by creating a narrative that resonates with the target audience. A well-crafted story can elicit emotions, build trust, and make a product more appealing by connecting it to the consumer's personal experiences.

The Role of Repetition

Repetition is a core strategy in advertising. By repeatedly exposing consumers to the same message, slogan, or visual, advertisers aim to reinforce brand recognition and make the product more familiar. This repetition can lead to what's known as the "mere exposure effect," where consumers develop a preference for a product simply because they have been exposed to it multiple times. For example, a jingle that is played over and over again in commercials can become stuck in a consumer's mind, making the brand more memorable. Over time, this familiarity can translate into trust and preference, leading to an increased likelihood of purchase.

Targeted Advertising

With the advent of digital technology, advertising has become more personalized and targeted. Companies now have access to vast amounts of consumer data, allowing them to create highly specific advertisements tailored to individual preferences, behaviours, and demographics. This means that consumers are often shown ads that are directly relevant to their interests, increasing the chances of conversion.

For instance, if consumers frequently search for fitness-related content online, they may start seeing ads for sports equipment, health supplements, or gym memberships. While targeted advertising can be convenient, it also raises concerns about privacy and the potential for manipulation. Consumers should be aware of how their data are used and consider the influence of targeted ads on their purchasing decisions.

The Long-Term Effects of Advertising

Advertising not only affects immediate buying habits but also has long-term effects on consumer behaviour and attitudes. Over time, continuous exposure to certain types of advertising can shape consumers' perceptions of what is normal or desirable. For example, ads that constantly promote luxury products or an idealized lifestyle can lead consumers to aspire to these standards, even if they are unrealistic or unattainable.

Moreover, advertising can influence societal values and norms, particularly in areas such as body image, gender roles, and consumerism. For instance, the portrayal of beauty in fashion ads can set standards that affect how people view themselves and others. Understanding these long-term effects can help consumers critically evaluate the messages they receive and make more conscious choices about the products they support.

Conclusion

Consumer behaviour is a complex field influenced by a myriad of psychological, social, economic, and technological factors. Advertising plays a significant role in shaping these behaviours by leveraging various techniques to persuade and influence consumer decisions. By understanding the underlying mechanisms that drive consumer behaviour, individuals can become more informed and empowered in their purchasing decisions.

Awareness of how advertising affects buying habits can help consumers resist manipulative tactics and make choices that align with their true needs and values. As the marketplace continues to evolve, with new forms of advertising and marketing emerging, the ability to critically assess and navigate these influences will become increasingly important for making sound economic decisions.

14.
THE ROLE OF TECHNOLOGY IN THE ECONOMY

Technology has always been a driving force behind economic change, reshaping industries, creating new markets, and influencing how businesses and consumers interact. In recent decades, the rapid pace of technological advancement has accelerated these changes, making it crucial to understand how technology impacts the economy. From the advent of the internet to the rise of automation and artificial intelligence, technology has transformed every aspect of economic life. This chapter explores the multifaceted role of technology in the economy, focusing on its effects on employment, the emergence of e-commerce, and the future of work in a digital age.

How Technological Advancements Affect Employment

Job Creation and Destruction

Technological advancements can be both a boon and a challenge for the job market. On one hand, new technologies create entirely new industries and job opportunities. For instance, the rise of the tech industry has led to the creation of millions of jobs in software development, cybersecurity, data analysis, and more. However, these same advancements can also render certain jobs obsolete. Automation and artificial intelligence, for example, are increasingly capable of performing tasks that were once the domain of human workers, leading to job displacement in sectors such as manufacturing and retail.

The Shift to High-Skill Jobs

As technology advances, there is a growing demand for workers with specialized skills. Jobs in the digital economy often require proficiency in areas such as coding, data science, and digital marketing. This shift has led to a growing divide between high-skill, high-paying jobs and low-skill, low-paying ones. Workers in traditional industries may find it challenging to transition to these new roles without significant retraining or education, exacerbating issues of income inequality and job insecurity.

Remote Work and the Gig Economy

Technology has also revolutionized the nature of work itself, enabling remote work and the rise of the gig economy. Platforms such as Upwork, Fiverr, and Uber allow individuals to work flexibly and independently, often from anywhere in the world. While this shift offers greater autonomy and work-life balance for some, it also raises concerns about job security, benefits, and the erosion of traditional employer-employee relationships.

The Rise of E-Commerce and Its Impact on Traditional Markets

The Growth of Online Shopping

E-commerce has dramatically altered the retail landscape. Online shopping platforms like Amazon, Alibaba, and eBay have revolutionized how consumers purchase goods and services. The convenience of shopping from home, coupled with the ability to compare prices and read reviews, has made e-commerce a dominant force in the global economy. This shift has put pressure on traditional brick-and-mortar stores, many of which have struggled to compete with the speed, variety, and often lower prices offered by online retailers.

The Impact on Local Businesses

The rise of e-commerce has had a significant impact on local businesses, particularly small retailers. As consumers increasingly turn to online platforms, many small businesses have seen a decline in foot traffic and sales. While some have successfully adapted by establishing an online presence or offering unique products and services that differentiate them from larger competitors, others have been forced to close their doors. This trend has reshaped the economic landscape of communities, leading to concerns about the loss of local culture and identity.

Changes in Supply Chain and Logistics

E-commerce has also transformed supply chain and logistics operations. The need for fast and reliable delivery has led to innovations in warehousing, transportation, and inventory management. Companies are now investing in advanced technologies such as drones, autonomous vehicles, and robotics to streamline operations and meet consumer demands for rapid delivery. These changes have created new opportunities in logistics and supply chain management but have also disrupted traditional industries such as trucking and warehousing.

The Future of Work in a Digital Age

The Role of Automation and AI:

Automation and artificial intelligence (AI) are poised to play a central role in the future of work. From automated manufacturing processes to AI-driven customer service bots, these technologies are already changing how businesses operate. While automation can increase efficiency and reduce costs, it also raises concerns about the displacement of workers and the need for new skills. The future workforce will likely require a higher level of technical expertise and adaptability to thrive in an increasingly automated economy.

The Importance of Lifelong Learning

In a rapidly changing technological landscape, the concept of lifelong learning is becoming increasingly important. Workers must continually update their skills to remain competitive in the job market. Governments, educational institutions, and employers will need to invest in reskilling and upskilling programs to help workers transition into new roles created by technological advancements. Lifelong learning will be essential for individuals to navigate the challenges and opportunities presented by the digital economy.

The Ethical Considerations of Technology

As technology continues to advance, ethical considerations will play a critical role in shaping the future of work. Issues such as data privacy, algorithmic bias, and the potential for job displacement must be addressed to ensure that technological progress benefits society as a whole. Policymakers, business leaders, and technologists will need to collaborate to create frameworks that balance innovation with social responsibility.

Conclusion

Technology has a profound impact on the economy, influencing everything from employment to consumer behaviour. As we move further into the digital age, understanding the role of technology in economic life will be essential for coping with the challenges and opportunities it presents. Whether it's adapting to new job markets, leveraging e-commerce for business success, or preparing for the future of work, individuals and organizations must stay informed and agile in a rapidly evolving landscape. The key to thriving in this environment will be a willingness to embrace change, invest in continuous learning, and consider the broader implications of technological progress.

15.
THE DIGITAL ECONOMY

The Growth of the Digital Marketplace

The Evolution of E-Commerce

The digital marketplace has grown exponentially over the past few decades, transforming how goods and services are bought and sold. The rise of the Internet has allowed businesses to reach a global audience, and e-commerce platforms such as Amazon, eBay, and Alibaba have become household names. What began as a convenient way to shop from home has now become a dominant force in the global economy. Online retail sales continue to rise, fueled by advancements in technology, increased internet penetration, and changing consumer preferences.

The Shift to Digital Services

The digital economy is not limited to the sale of physical goods. The rise of digital services has been equally transformative. Streaming platforms like Netflix and Spotify, cloud computing services like AWS, and gig economy platforms like Uber and Airbnb are examples of how the digital marketplace has expanded beyond traditional retail. These services offer convenience, accessibility, and often lower costs, making them increasingly popular among consumers. The shift to digital services has also created new opportunities for entrepreneurs and businesses to innovate and reach new markets.

The Role of Data and Analytics

One of the most significant drivers of the digital marketplace is the use of data and analytics. Companies now collect vast amounts of data on consumer behaviour, preferences, and trends, which they use to tailor their offerings and improve customer experiences. Data analytics allows businesses to make informed decisions, optimize their operations, and gain a competitive edge. However, the increasing reliance on data also raises concerns about privacy, security, and the ethical use of information.

Cryptocurrency and Digital Payments

The Rise of Cryptocurrencies

Cryptocurrencies, such as Bitcoin, Ethereum, and Ripple, have emerged as a new form of digital currency that operates independently of traditional financial institutions. These decentralized currencies are based on blockchain technology, which provides transparency, security, and immutability. Cryptocurrencies offer an alternative to traditional banking systems, enabling peer-to-peer transactions across borders without the need for intermediaries. While still relatively new, cryptocurrencies have gained traction among investors, tech enthusiasts, and even some mainstream businesses.

The Evolution of Digital Payments

The digital economy has also seen significant advancements in payment methods. Digital payments, including mobile payments, e-wallets, and contactless transactions, have become increasingly common. Services like PayPal, Apple Pay, and Google Wallet allow consumers to make purchases with just a few taps on their smartphones. These payment methods offer convenience, speed, and security, making them popular choices for both online and in-store transactions. The COVID-19 pandemic further accelerated the adoption of digital payments, as consumers sought contactless options to reduce the risk of virus transmission.

The Potential and Challenges of Cryptocurrency

While cryptocurrencies hold great potential, they also face several challenges. Volatility is one of the most significant issues, with prices often experiencing dramatic fluctuations. Regulatory uncertainty is another concern, as governments and financial institutions grapple with how to classify and regulate these digital assets. Additionally, the energy consumption associated with cryptocurrency mining has raised environmental concerns. Despite these challenges, cryptocurrencies continue to evolve, with some predicting they could play a more prominent role in the global economy in the future.

The Impact of Digitalization on Traditional Industries

Disruption of Established Business Models

Digitalization has disrupted traditional industries, forcing businesses to adapt or risk becoming obsolete. Retail is a prime example, where brick-and-mortar stores have faced intense competition from online retailers. The media and entertainment industry has also been transformed by digitalization, with streaming services and social media platforms challenging traditional television and print media. In finance, fintech companies are revolutionizing banking and investment services, offering more accessible and user-friendly alternatives to traditional banks.

The Role of Automation and AI

Automation and artificial intelligence (AI) are playing an increasingly important role in the digital economy. From manufacturing to customer service, AI-driven technologies are streamlining operations, reducing costs, and improving efficiency. In the automotive industry, for example, self-driving cars are being developed that could eventually replace traditional vehicles. In healthcare, AI is being used to diagnose diseases, develop personalized treatment plans, and even assist in surgeries. While these advancements offer significant benefits, they also raise concerns about job displacement and the need for new skills in the workforce.

The Importance of Digital Transformation

For traditional industries to survive and thrive in the digital economy, digital transformation is essential. This involves integrating digital technologies into all aspects of a business, from operations to customer interactions. Companies that embrace digital transformation can improve their efficiency, reach new markets, and enhance customer experiences. However, the process can be challenging, requiring significant investment, cultural shifts, and the development of new capabilities. Those that succeed in digital transformation will be better positioned to compete in the rapidly evolving digital economy.

Conclusion

The digital economy is reshaping the world, creating new opportunities and challenges for businesses and consumers alike. The growth of the digital marketplace, the rise of cryptocurrencies and digital payments, and the impact of digitalization on traditional industries are all testament to the transformative power of technology. As we move forward, understanding and adapting to the digital economy will be crucial for success. Whether it's embracing new payment methods, leveraging data analytics, or undergoing digital transformation, businesses and individuals must stay informed and agile in this ever-changing landscape. The future of the economy is digital, and those who are prepared will be best equipped to thrive.

16.
HEALTHCARE ECONOMICS

The Cost of Healthcare and Its Economic Impact

Rising Healthcare Costs

Healthcare costs have been on a steady rise globally, impacting both individuals and economies at large. Factors contributing to this increase include advancements in medical technology, the rising cost of prescription drugs, an aging population, and the administrative costs associated with healthcare services. As healthcare becomes more expensive, it places a greater financial burden on individuals, families, and governments, often leading to difficult choices regarding treatment and care.

Economic Consequences of High Healthcare Costs

The high cost of healthcare can have profound economic consequences. For individuals, it can lead to financial hardship, especially for those without adequate health insurance. Many people are forced to make trade-offs, such as choosing between healthcare and other essential needs like housing or education. On a broader scale, rising healthcare costs can strain government budgets, diverting funds from other critical areas like infrastructure and education. Additionally, businesses may face higher costs in providing health benefits to employees, potentially impacting wages and job creation.

Healthcare Costs and Economic Inequality

Healthcare costs contribute to economic inequality, as those with lower incomes are often less able to afford necessary care. This can lead to disparities in health outcomes, where wealthier individuals have access to better care and live longer, healthier lives. The economic impact of this inequality is significant, as poor health can reduce productivity, increase absenteeism, and limit opportunities for upward mobility. Addressing these disparities is crucial for creating a more equitable and economically stable society.

Understanding Health Insurance

The Basics of Health Insurance

Health insurance is a system designed to help individuals manage the financial risk associated with healthcare costs. By paying regular premiums, individuals and families can access a range of healthcare services without bearing the full cost out of pocket. Health insurance can be provided by employers, purchased individually, or provided by the government, depending on the country and healthcare system in place.

Types of Health Insurance Plans

Health insurance plans come in various forms, each with its own set of benefits and limitations. Common types include Health Maintenance Organizations (HMOs), Preferred Provider Organizations (PPOs), and high-deductible health plans. HMOs typically require members to choose a primary care physician and obtain referrals for specialist care, while PPOs offer more flexibility in choosing healthcare providers. High-deductible plans often have lower premiums but higher out-of-pocket costs, making them suitable for individuals who prefer to pay lower premiums and are less likely to need frequent care.

The Role of Health Insurance in Access to Care

Health insurance plays a critical role in determining access to healthcare. Those with insurance are more likely to receive preventive care, early diagnosis, and timely treatment, leading to better health outcomes. Conversely, individuals without insurance may delay or forgo necessary care owing to cost concerns, resulting in more severe health issues and higher long-term costs. Ensuring that more people have access to affordable health insurance is essential for improving public health and reducing the overall economic burden of healthcare.

Challenges in the Health Insurance Market

The health insurance market faces several challenges, including rising premiums, the complexity of plans, and the issue of coverage gaps. Premiums have increased in recent years, making it more difficult for individuals and families to afford coverage. Additionally, the complexity of health insurance plans can make it challenging for consumers to understand their options and make informed decisions. Coverage gaps, where individuals are temporarily uninsured, can also lead to financial instability and reduced access to care.

The Role of Government in Healthcare

Government's Role in Providing Healthcare:

Governments play a significant role in the healthcare system, from providing direct care through public healthcare systems to regulating private healthcare providers and insurers. In many countries, the government is responsible for ensuring that all citizens have access to healthcare, regardless of their ability to pay. This can involve funding public hospitals, subsidizing health insurance, and implementing policies to control healthcare costs.

Public Healthcare Systems

Public healthcare systems, such as the National Health Service (NHS) in the UK or Medicare in Australia, are funded by taxpayer money and provide healthcare services to citizens at little or no cost. These systems aim to ensure that everyone has access to essential healthcare services, regardless of income. Public healthcare systems can help reduce the economic burden of healthcare on individuals, but they also face challenges such as long wait times, limited resources, and the need for sustainable funding.

Government Regulation of Healthcare

In addition to providing healthcare, governments regulate the healthcare industry to ensure safety, quality, and fairness. This can include setting standards for medical care, approving new drugs and treatments, and overseeing health insurance markets. Government regulation is essential for protecting consumers from fraud, ensuring that healthcare providers meet quality standards, and promoting competition in the market. However, excessive regulation can also stifle innovation and increase costs.

The Debate Over Government's Role in Healthcare

The extent of government involvement in healthcare is a topic of ongoing debate. Advocates for greater government involvement argue that healthcare is a fundamental right and that public systems ensure equitable access to care. They also contend that government regulation is necessary to control costs and protect consumers. Opponents, however, argue that government-run healthcare systems can be inefficient, limit choice, and stifle innovation. They advocate for a more market-driven approach, where competition and consumer choice drive improvements in quality and cost.

Conclusion

Healthcare economics is a complex and multifaceted field that touches every aspect of our lives. The rising cost of healthcare, the role of health insurance, and the involvement of government all play crucial roles in shaping how we access and afford healthcare. As the healthcare landscape continues to evolve, it is essential for individuals, policymakers, and businesses to understand these dynamics to make informed decisions that promote both economic stability and public health. Balancing cost, access, and quality in healthcare is a challenge, but it is one that must be addressed to ensure a healthier and more prosperous future for all.

17.
HOUSING AND REAL ESTATE

The Economics of Buying vs. Renting

Deciding Between Buying and Renting

One of the most significant financial decisions individuals and families face is whether to buy a home or rent. Each option has its own set of advantages and disadvantages, influenced by factors such as financial stability, lifestyle preferences, and long-term goals. Buying a home often appeals to those who desire stability and see property ownership as an investment. Renting, on the other hand, offers flexibility and can be a better choice for those who may need to relocate frequently or who are not ready for the financial responsibilities of homeownership.

The Financial Implications of Buying

Buying a home requires a substantial upfront investment, including a down payment, closing costs, and ongoing expenses such as property taxes, insurance, and maintenance. However, homeownership allows individuals to build equity over time, as property values typically appreciate. Additionally, homeowners may benefit from tax deductions on mortgage interest and property taxes. The financial benefits of buying can make it a good long-term investment, but it also comes with risks, such as market fluctuations and the potential for unexpected expenses.

The Costs and Benefits of Renting

Renting offers lower upfront costs and fewer responsibilities compared to buying. Renters are not responsible for property maintenance or repairs, and they are not exposed to the risks of declining property values. However, renting does not provide the opportunity to build equity, and rent payments may increase over time. Renters also face the possibility of having to move if their lease is not renewed or if the property is sold. Despite these drawbacks, renting can be an attractive option for those who prioritize flexibility and do not want to be tied down to a specific location.

Economic Factors Influencing the Decision

Economic conditions, such as interest rates, housing market trends, and job stability, play a significant role in the decision to buy or rent. For example, when interest rates are low, borrowing costs decrease, making homeownership more affordable. Conversely, in a competitive housing market with rapidly rising prices, renting may be more financially prudent. Additionally, personal economic factors, such as income stability and debt levels, should be carefully considered when deciding between buying and renting.

Understanding Mortgages and Interest Rates

What Is a Mortgage?

A mortgage is a loan used to purchase real estate, with the property itself serving as collateral. Mortgages allow individuals to buy homes without paying the full purchase price upfront. Instead, they make monthly payments over a specified period, typically 15 to 30 years, until the loan is fully repaid. Mortgages are a common financing option for homebuyers, but they come with significant long-term financial commitments and responsibilities.

Types of Mortgages

There are several types of mortgages, each with its own features and requirements. Fixed-rate mortgages have a consistent interest rate and monthly payment throughout the loan term, providing stability and predictability. Adjustable-rate mortgages (ARMs), on the other hand, have interest rates that can change over time, typically starting with a lower rate that may increase after an initial period. Other options include government-backed loans, such as FHA loans, which are designed to help first-time buyers with lower down payment requirements.

The Role of Interest Rates in Mortgages

Interest rates are a crucial factor in determining the affordability of a mortgage. Lower interest rates reduce the cost of borrowing, making monthly payments more manageable and increasing the amount of homebuyers can afford. Conversely, higher interest rates increase the cost of borrowing, leading to higher monthly payments and potentially limiting buyers' purchasing power. Interest rates are influenced by a variety of factors, including inflation, economic growth, and central bank policies. Homebuyers should carefully consider interest rate trends when choosing a mortgage.

The Impact of Mortgage Terms

The length of the mortgage term also affects monthly payments and the total cost of the loan. Shorter-term mortgages, such as 15-year loans, typically have higher monthly payments but lower total interest costs, as the loan is repaid more quickly. Longer-term mortgages, such as 30-year loans, have lower monthly payments but result in higher total interest costs over the life of the loan. Borrowers must weigh the benefits of lower monthly payments against the higher long-term costs when selecting a mortgage term.

The Impact of the Housing Market on the Economy

The Housing Market as an Economic Indicator

The housing market is a critical component of the overall economy, serving as both a leading indicator and a driver of economic activity. Strong housing markets often signal economic growth, as rising home prices boost consumer wealth and confidence, leading to increased spending and investment. Conversely, a weak housing market can indicate economic challenges, as declining home values reduce household wealth and can lead to reduced consumer spending, slower economic growth, and increased financial instability.

The Ripple Effects of Housing on Other Sectors

The housing market's influence extends beyond just real estate transactions. It affects a wide range of industries, including construction, manufacturing, finance, and retail. For example, a booming housing market drives demand for construction materials, home furnishings, and appliances, creating jobs and boosting economic output. The financial sector is also closely tied to the housing market, as mortgage lending and real estate investments play a significant role in banking profitability. Changes in the housing market can have far-reaching effects on the broader economy.

The Role of Government Policies in the Housing Market

Government policies can have a significant impact on the housing market, influencing everything from homeownership rates to housing affordability. Policies such as mortgage interest rate deductions, tax incentives for homebuyers, and affordable housing programs can encourage homeownership and stimulate the housing market. Conversely, regulations and zoning laws can restrict housing supply, driving up prices and limiting access to affordable housing. Governments play a crucial role in balancing the goals of promoting homeownership, ensuring housing affordability, and maintaining economic stability.

Housing Bubbles and Economic Crises

Housing bubbles, characterized by rapid and unsustainable increases in home prices, can have devastating economic consequences when they burst. The global financial crisis of 2008 is a prime example, where a collapse in the U.S. housing market led to widespread mortgage defaults, bank failures, and a severe economic downturn. Understanding the risks of housing bubbles and the importance of sound lending practices is crucial for maintaining a stable and healthy housing market. Policymakers, lenders, and consumers must all be vigilant to avoid the excesses that can lead to economic crises.

Conclusion

Housing and real estate play a central role in both individual financial well-being and the broader economy. The decisions to buy or rent, the intricacies of mortgages, and the dynamics of the housing market all have far-reaching implications. Understanding these factors is essential for making informed decisions that align with long-term financial goals. Additionally, recognizing the impact of the housing market on the economy underscores the importance of responsible policies and practices in maintaining economic stability and promoting access to affordable housing for all.

18.
THE ECONOMICS OF EDUCATION

The Cost of Education and Its Return on Investment

Understanding the Financial Costs of Education

Education, especially higher education, represents one of the most significant financial investments that individuals and families make. The costs include tuition, fees, books, and living expenses, which can add up to substantial amounts over the years. With the rising cost of college and university education, understanding the financial commitment involved is crucial for students and their families. Beyond the direct costs, there are also opportunity costs, such as the income a student might forgo while pursuing a degree instead of working full-time.

Evaluating the Return on Investment (ROI) in Education

The return on investment (ROI) of education is a key consideration when assessing the value of this financial commitment. While the upfront costs can be high, education generally provides a substantial long-term economic benefit in the form of higher earnings, better job opportunities, and increased job security. On average, individuals with higher levels of education tend to earn more over their lifetimes than those with only a high school diploma. However, the ROI can vary widely depending on factors such as the field of study, the institution attended, and the job market conditions at the time of graduation.

Comparing Costs and ROI Across Different Fields of Study

Different fields of study offer varying levels of economic return. For example, degrees in STEM (Science, Technology, Engineering, and Mathematics) fields tend to have higher average salaries and stronger job prospects compared to degrees in the humanities or arts. However, the value of education is not solely economic; personal passion, fulfillment, and societal contributions also play important roles. Students should weigh both financial and personal factors when choosing a field of study to ensure that their educational investment aligns with their long-term goals.

The Long-Term Impact of Education on Earnings:

Education has a profound impact on long-term earning potential. Studies consistently show that higher education levels correlate with higher median earnings. This financial advantage often grows over time, as individuals with higher education levels are more likely to receive promotions and salary increases. Additionally, education can provide a buffer against economic downturns, as those with higher education levels typically experience lower unemployment rates and greater job stability. The long-term financial benefits of education highlight its importance as an investment in one's future.

Student Loans and Financial Aid

Navigating the Landscape of Student Loans

For many students, taking out loans is a necessary step to afford the cost of higher education. Understanding the different types of student loans—federal versus private, subsidized versus unsubsidized—is critical for making informed borrowing decisions. Federal student loans often offer more favourable terms, such as lower interest rates and flexible repayment options, compared to private loans. However, borrowing to finance education also means taking on debt that must be repaid, which can have long-term financial implications.

The Impact of Student Debt on Financial Well-Being

Student debt has become a significant financial burden for millions of graduates. The rising cost of education has led to increased borrowing, and many students graduate with substantial debt. This debt can impact financial decisions for years to come, affecting everything from career choices to homeownership and retirement savings. High levels of student debt can also limit economic mobility, as graduates may delay major life milestones, such as starting a family or buying a home, owing to financial constraints.

Exploring Financial Aid Options

In addition to student loans, there are various forms of financial aid available to help offset the cost of education. Scholarships, grants, and work-study programs provide financial assistance that does not require repayment, making them highly valuable for students. Understanding how to apply for financial aid, including completing the Free Application for Federal Student Aid (FAFSA) and exploring scholarship opportunities, is essential for minimizing the need for student loans. Financial aid can significantly reduce the overall cost of education and make it more accessible to students from diverse economic backgrounds.

Strategies for Managing Student Debt

Managing student debt effectively is crucial for maintaining financial health after graduation. Strategies include understanding repayment options, such as income-driven repayment plans, which adjust monthly payments based on income, and exploring loan forgiveness programs available for certain professions or public service work. Additionally, budgeting and financial planning can help graduates make timely payments and avoid default, which can have severe consequences on credit scores and financial opportunities. Proactively managing student debt can help graduates achieve financial stability and focus on long-term financial goals.

The Role of Education in Economic Mobility

Education as a Pathway to Economic Mobility

Education is often seen as a key driver of economic mobility, providing individuals with the skills and knowledge needed to improve their economic standing. For many, education offers a pathway out of poverty and into higher-paying jobs and greater financial security. Access to quality education can level the playing field, allowing individuals from all backgrounds to compete for opportunities that can significantly change their economic trajectory. The role of education in fostering upward mobility underscores its importance as a public good and a vital component of economic development.

The Relationship Between Education and Income Inequality

Education plays a critical role in addressing income inequality by providing individuals with the tools needed to secure better-paying jobs and climb the economic ladder. However, disparities in access to quality education can perpetuate income inequality, as those from wealthier backgrounds often have greater access to educational resources and opportunities. Ensuring equitable access to education is essential for reducing income inequality and promoting economic mobility for all individuals, regardless of their socioeconomic status.

The Economic Benefits of Investing in Education

Investing in education yields significant economic benefits for both individuals and society as a whole. Educated individuals are more likely to contribute to economic growth through higher productivity, innovation, and entrepreneurship. Additionally, higher education levels are associated with lower crime rates, better health outcomes, and greater civic engagement, all of which have positive economic implications. Public investments in education, from early childhood through higher education, are crucial for building a skilled workforce and fostering long-term economic prosperity.

Addressing Barriers to Educational Access

Despite the significant benefits of education, barriers to access remain for many individuals, particularly those from low-income or marginalized communities. These barriers include financial constraints, lack of access to quality schools, and social factors such as discrimination or family responsibilities. Addressing these barriers is essential for ensuring that all individuals have the opportunity to benefit from education and achieve economic mobility. Policies that expand access to financial aid, support early childhood education, and improve the quality of public schools are critical for creating a more equitable and inclusive educational system.

Conclusion

Education is a powerful tool for economic empowerment, offering individuals the knowledge and skills needed to navigate the complexities of the modern economy. While the costs of education can be high, the long-term return on investment makes it a worthwhile pursuit for those seeking to improve their economic prospects. Understanding the financial aspects of education, including the implications of student loans and the potential for economic mobility, is crucial for making informed decisions. By addressing barriers to access and ensuring that education remains a pathway to opportunity for all, we can build a more equitable and prosperous society.

19.
ENVIRONMENTAL ECONOMICS

The Economic Impact of Environmental Policies

Understanding Environmental Policies and Their Purpose

Environmental policies are regulations and laws enacted by governments to protect natural resources, reduce pollution, and promote sustainable practices. These policies aim to mitigate the negative impacts of economic activities on the environment by setting standards for emissions, waste management, and resource use. Examples include carbon taxes, emissions trading systems, and regulations on industrial pollution. The purpose of these policies is to ensure that economic growth does not come at the expense of environmental degradation, thereby safeguarding the planet for future generations.

The Costs and Benefits of Environmental Regulations

Implementing environmental policies often involves significant costs for businesses and governments.

Companies may need to invest in new technologies, modify production processes, or comply with stringent regulations, all of which can increase operational costs. Governments may need to allocate resources for monitoring, enforcement, and incentives for green practices. However, the benefits of these policies often outweigh the costs, as they lead to healthier ecosystems, improved public health, and long-term economic sustainability. Moreover, environmental regulations can drive innovation, creating new markets and job opportunities in green industries.

The Impact on Industries and Employment

Environmental policies can have varying impacts on different industries. Sectors that are heavily reliant on natural resources or that produce high levels of pollution, such as manufacturing, energy, and agriculture, may face greater challenges in adapting to new regulations. In some cases, this can lead to job losses or shifts in employment patterns. However, other sectors, particularly those involved in renewable energy, waste management, and environmental consulting, may experience growth and increased demand for skilled workers. The overall impact on employment depends on the balance between job losses in traditional industries and job creation in emerging green sectors.

Global Environmental Policies and Their Economic Implications

Environmental policies are increasingly being coordinated at the global level, as environmental issues such as climate change, deforestation, and ocean pollution cross national borders. International agreements like the Paris Agreement on climate change set targets for reducing greenhouse gas emissions and encourage countries to adopt sustainable practices. While these agreements are crucial for addressing global environmental challenges, they also have significant economic implications. Countries that are major polluters may face economic pressures to reduce emissions, while developing nations may require financial assistance and technology transfer to implement sustainable practices.

The Cost of Sustainable Practices

The Financial Implications of Adopting Sustainable Practices

Sustainability often comes with upfront costs, whether for businesses, governments, or individuals. Companies may need to invest in energy-efficient technologies, reduce waste, or source materials from sustainable suppliers. These investments can be substantial, particularly for small and medium-sized enterprises (SMEs). However, the long-term financial benefits, such as reduced energy costs, improved brand reputation, and compliance with regulations, can make sustainability a profitable endeavour over time. For governments, the cost of promoting sustainability can include subsidies for renewable energy, investments in public transportation, and funding for research and development in green technologies.

The Role of Corporate Social Responsibility (CSR) in Promoting Sustainability

Corporate Social Responsibility (CSR) has become a key aspect of modern business, with many companies recognizing the importance of integrating sustainable practices into their operations. CSR initiatives often focus on reducing environmental impact, such as minimizing carbon footprints, conserving water, and promoting recycling. While these initiatives can be costly, they also offer significant benefits, including enhanced brand loyalty, increased investor confidence, and access to new markets. Moreover, companies that prioritize sustainability may be better positioned to attract and retain talent, as more employees seek to work for socially responsible organizations.

The Economic Case for Sustainable Consumer Choices

Consumers also play a crucial role in driving sustainability through their purchasing decisions. Sustainable products, such as organic food, eco-friendly packaging, and energy-efficient appliances, often come with higher price tags. However, consumers who prioritize sustainability are willing to pay a premium for products that align with their values. This demand creates economic incentives for companies to adopt sustainable practices and develop green products. Additionally, sustainable consumer choices can lead to long-term savings, such as lower energy bills or reduced waste disposal costs, further reinforcing the economic case for sustainability.

The Long-Term Economic Benefits of Sustainability

While the initial costs of sustainability can be high, the long-term economic benefits are significant. Sustainable practices help conserve resources, reduce environmental degradation, and mitigate the impacts of climate change, all of which contribute to economic stability. For businesses, sustainability can lead to increased efficiency, reduced risks, and access to new markets. For governments, promoting sustainability can enhance public health, reduce healthcare costs, and create resilient communities. Ultimately, the long-term economic benefits of sustainability outweigh the short-term costs, making it a sound investment for the future.

Balancing Economic Growth with Environmental Responsibility

The Challenge of Sustainable Economic Growth

Achieving economic growth while protecting the environment is a complex challenge that requires careful planning and coordination. Traditional models of economic growth have often prioritized industrialization, resource extraction, and consumption, leading to environmental degradation. However, as the impacts of climate change and resource depletion become more apparent, there is a growing recognition that sustainable economic growth is essential for long-term prosperity. This requires a shift towards green growth strategies that prioritize environmental protection, resource efficiency, and social equity.

Strategies for Integrating Environmental Responsibility into Economic Planning

Governments and businesses are increasingly exploring ways to integrate environmental responsibility into economic planning. This can involve adopting policies that promote green technologies, incentivizing sustainable practices, and implementing measures to reduce carbon emissions. Economic planning that takes into account environmental considerations can help mitigate the negative impacts of economic activities on the environment while ensuring that growth is sustainable. Examples include the development of green infrastructure, the promotion of circular economies (which involves sharing, leasing, reusing, repairing, refurbishing, and recycling existing materials and products as long as possible), and the implementation of sustainable urban planning.

The Role of Innovation in Achieving Sustainable Growth

Innovation is a key driver of sustainable economic growth. Advances in technology, such as renewable energy, electric vehicles, and smart grids, offer new opportunities to reduce environmental impact while supporting economic development. Additionally, innovation in business models, such as the sharing economy and circular economy, can promote resource efficiency and reduce waste. Governments and businesses that invest in innovation are better positioned to achieve sustainable growth, create new markets, and drive economic development while minimizing environmental harm.

The Importance of Collaboration in Balancing Growth and Responsibility

Balancing economic growth with environmental responsibility requires collaboration between governments, businesses, and civil society. Governments play a crucial role in setting policies and regulations that promote sustainability, while businesses must adopt practices that minimize environmental impact. Civil society, including non-governmental organizations (NGOs) and consumers, can advocate for sustainable practices and hold businesses and governments accountable. Collaborative efforts, such as public-private partnerships and international agreements, are essential for addressing global environmental challenges and achieving sustainable economic growth.

Conclusion

Environmental economics highlights the interconnectedness of economic activities and environmental sustainability. The economic impact of environmental policies, the cost of sustainable practices, and the challenge of balancing growth with responsibility are all critical considerations in today's global economy. By understanding these dynamics, individuals, businesses, and governments can make informed decisions that contribute to a more sustainable future. Sustainable economic growth is not only achievable but essential for ensuring the well-being of current and future generations.

20.
MAKING INFORMED ECONOMIC DECISIONS

How to Analyze Economic Data

Understanding economic data is the first step toward making informed economic decisions. The vast array of data available—from government reports to market analyses—can seem overwhelming. However, you can break down complex information into actionable insights by developing a systematic approach to data analysis.

Start by identifying the source of the data. Reliable sources such as government agencies, reputable financial institutions, and well-known economic research organizations should be your go-to for accurate and unbiased information. Always check the date of the data to ensure they are current and relevant to your decision-making process.

Next, focus on the key metrics that are most relevant to your decision. For example, if you're evaluating the state of the housing market, look at data on home prices, mortgage rates, and housing starts. If you're considering a job change, pay attention to employment rates, wage growth, and industry-specific trends.

Once you've gathered the necessary data, it's crucial to analyze them in context. Consider and compare historical trends with current figures to identify patterns or anomalies. Use tools like graphs, charts, and statistical models to visualize the data and make them easier to interpret.

Finally, integrate qualitative information with your quantitative analysis. Economic data often tell only part of the story; qualitative factors like consumer sentiment, geopolitical events, and technological advancements can significantly impact economic outcomes. By considering both qualitative and quantitative data, you can make more well-rounded and informed decisions.

Understanding Economic Indicators

Economic indicators are statistics that provide insight into the overall health and direction of an economy. They are essential tools for making informed economic decisions, whether you're an individual investor, a business owner, or a policy-maker.

There are three main types of economic indicators: leading, lagging, and coincident. **Leading indicators**, such as stock market returns, consumer confidence, and new business start-ups, provide early signals of where the economy is headed. They are particularly useful for making predictions and preparing for future economic conditions.

Lagging indicators, such as unemployment rates, inflation rates, and corporate earnings, confirm trends that are already in place. These indicators are valuable for assessing the effectiveness of past decisions and for making adjustments to strategies based on recent economic performance.

Coincident indicators, like gross domestic product (GDP)—the market value of all final goods and services produced, retail sales, and industrial production, move in line with the overall economy. They provide a real-time snapshot of economic activity and are useful for understanding the current state of the economy.

To effectively use economic indicators in decision-making, it's important to understand how they interact with each other. For example, a rise in leading indicators like consumer confidence might suggest a future increase in GDP, a coincident indicator. On the other hand, a spike in inflation, a lagging indicator, might signal the need to adjust investment strategies to protect against eroding purchasing power.

By staying informed about key economic indicators and understanding their implications, you can make more strategic decisions that align with the broader economic landscape.

Applying Economic Principles to Everyday Decisions

Economic principles are not just abstract theories; they are practical tools that can be applied to everyday decisions. Whether you're budgeting for your household, planning a major purchase, or investing in your future, economic principles can help you make smarter, more informed choices.

One of the most fundamental principles in economics is the concept of opportunity cost. Every decision you make has a cost, which is the next best alternative you forego. Understanding opportunity cost can help you weigh your options more carefully and choose the one that offers the greatest value. For example, when deciding whether to spend money on a vacation or invest it in a retirement account, considering the opportunity cost can clarify which option better aligns with your long-term goals.

Another important principle is the law of supply and demand, which affects the prices of goods and services. By understanding how supply and demand influence prices, you can make more informed decisions about when to buy or sell. For instance, purchasing seasonal items off-season when demand is low can save you money, while understanding demand trends can help you time investments more effectively.

The principle of marginal analysis is also valuable in everyday decision-making. Marginal analysis involves comparing the additional benefits of an action to its additional costs. This principle can be applied to decisions like whether to take on extra work for overtime pay or invest in further education. By focusing on the marginal benefits and costs, you can make decisions that maximize your overall well-being.

Finally, consider the principle of diversification in your financial decisions. Just as businesses diversify their product lines to reduce risk, you can diversify your investments to protect against market volatility. Diversification spreads risk across different assets, such as stocks, bonds, and real estate, reducing the impact of a downturn in any single market.

By applying these and other economic principles to your everyday decisions, you can make choices that are not only more informed but also more aligned with your financial goals and overall well-being.

21.
RETIREMENT PLANNING AND SOCIAL SECURITY

Understanding Social Security Benefits

Social Security is a vital component of retirement planning for many people. Understanding how it works, when to claim benefits, and how to maximize your benefits is essential for securing your financial future.

Social Security benefits are based on your earnings history, with higher lifetime earnings resulting in higher benefits. To qualify for benefits, you must have earned a minimum number of credits, which are accumulated based on your work history. Typically, in the United States, 40 credits (equivalent to 10 years of work) are required to qualify for retirement benefits.

The age at which you claim Social Security significantly impacts the amount you receive. You can begin claiming benefits as early as age 62, but doing so will permanently reduce your monthly benefit. Full retirement age (FRA) varies depending on your birth year, typically ranging between 66 and 67. If you delay claiming benefits past your FRA, your monthly benefit increases until age 70 when the maximum benefit is reached.

In addition to retirement benefits, Social Security provides spousal and survivor benefits. Spousal benefits allow a lower-earning spouse to receive up to 50% of the higher-earning spouse's benefit. Survivor benefits provide financial support to the surviving spouse and dependents of a deceased worker, helping him or her maintain financial stability during difficult times.

To maximize your Social Security benefits, consider factors such as your health, financial needs, and life expectancy. If you expect to live a long life, delaying benefits can result in a higher lifetime payout. On the other hand, if you need the income sooner or have health concerns, claiming benefits earlier might be the better choice.

Understanding your Social Security benefits and how to optimize them is crucial for ensuring that this important source of retirement income supports your long-term financial goals.

Planning for Retirement: Saving Strategies and Investment Options

Retirement planning goes beyond Social Security; it requires a comprehensive approach to saving and investing to ensure financial security in your later years. With rising life expectancies and the potential for increased healthcare costs, it's more important than ever to develop a robust retirement plan.

The first step in retirement planning is setting clear goals. Determine how much income you'll need in retirement by considering your current expenses, potential healthcare costs, and desired lifestyle. Use retirement calculators to estimate the total savings required to achieve these goals.

Next, explore various retirement savings options, such as employer-sponsored plans like 401(k)s, Individual Retirement Accounts (IRAs), and Roth IRAs. Employer-sponsored plans often come with matching contributions, which can significantly boost your savings. IRAs offer tax advantages, with traditional IRAs providing tax-deferred growth and Roth IRAs offering tax-free withdrawals in retirement. These plans exist in the United States, but similar plans may be available in other countries. For example, Canada has a Registered Retirement Savings Plan (RRSP).

Diversification is key to a successful retirement savings strategy. Spread your investments across different asset classes, such as stocks, bonds, and real estate, to reduce risk and increase potential returns. As you near retirement, consider shifting to a more conservative investment approach to protect your savings from market volatility.

Another critical aspect of retirement planning is managing debt. Paying off high-interest debt before retirement can free up more of your income for savings and reduce financial stress in retirement. Additionally, consider downsizing your home or relocating to a more affordable area to lower living expenses.

Regularly review and adjust your retirement plan as your financial situation and goals evolve. Keep track of your savings progress, reassess your investment strategy, and stay informed about changes in tax laws and Social Security benefits that could impact your retirement income.

By adopting a proactive approach to saving and investing, you can build a retirement plan that provides the financial security and peace of mind you need to enjoy your golden years.

The Future of Retirement in an Aging Society

As the global population ages, the concept of retirement is undergoing significant changes. Longer life expectancies, evolving workforce dynamics, and shifting economic conditions are shaping the future of retirement in ways that demand careful consideration and planning.

One of the most significant challenges of an aging society is the strain on Social Security and pension systems. With fewer workers supporting a growing number of retirees, there is increasing concern about the sustainability of these programs. Policymakers may need to consider raising the retirement age, adjusting benefit formulas, or implementing other reforms to ensure the long-term viability of Social Security.

The future of retirement also involves rethinking traditional notions of work and leisure. As people live longer, healthier lives, many are choosing to work beyond the traditional retirement age, either out of financial necessity or a desire to stay active and engaged. This trend, known as "phased retirement," allows individuals to gradually reduce their work hours while still earning an income and contributing to their savings.

Technological advancements are also playing a role in shaping the future of retirement. Automation and artificial intelligence may reduce the demand for certain types of jobs while creating new opportunities in other sectors. Lifelong learning and skills development will become increasingly important as workers adapt to these changes and seek new ways to remain relevant in the workforce.

Healthcare costs are another critical factor in retirement planning, as medical expenses tend to rise with age. The future of retirement will likely involve a greater emphasis on long-term care planning, with individuals and families needing to prepare for the potential costs of extended care, whether through savings, insurance, or other means.

Finally, the concept of retirement itself may continue to evolve, with more people seeking flexible, purpose-driven lifestyles that blend work, leisure, and community involvement. This shift could lead to new models of retirement living, such as co-housing communities, multigenerational living arrangements, and increased use of technology to stay connected and engaged.

The future of retirement in an aging society presents both challenges and opportunities. By staying informed, planning ahead, and embracing new possibilities, you can navigate this changing landscape and create a fulfilling and financially secure retirement.

22.
THE FUTURE OF WORK

The world of work is undergoing a profound transformation, driven by technological advancements, changing societal norms, and evolving economic conditions. The traditional 9-to-5 job, with its fixed location and long-term employment contracts, is giving way to more flexible, dynamic, and technology-driven models. This chapter explores the future of work, focusing on key trends such as the rise of remote and gig work, the impact of automation and artificial intelligence (AI) on employment, and how individuals and organizations can prepare for the workforce of the future.

The Rise of Remote and Gig Work

The Evolution of Workplaces

The COVID-19 pandemic accelerated a shift that was already underway: the move from traditional office-based work to remote and flexible working arrangements. With the advent of high-speed internet, cloud computing, and collaboration tools, employees can now work from virtually anywhere, breaking the geographic barriers that once defined employment.

Remote work offers numerous benefits, including increased work-life balance, reduced commuting time, and access to a broader talent pool. However, it also presents challenges, such as maintaining team cohesion, managing remote workers, and addressing cybersecurity concerns.

The Growth of the Gig Economy

Parallel to the rise of remote work is the expansion of the gig economy, characterized by short-term contracts, freelance work, and independent contracting. Platforms like Uber, Airbnb, and Upwork have revolutionized how people find work, enabling individuals to monetize their skills and assets in new ways.

The gig economy offers flexibility and autonomy but also raises questions about job security, benefits, and worker rights. As more people turn to gig work as a primary or supplementary source of income, the traditional employer-employee relationship is being redefined.

Balancing Flexibility and Security

The rise of remote and gig work requires a new approach to balancing flexibility with security. Workers must take a proactive role in managing their careers, seeking out continuous learning opportunities, and ensuring they have access to essential benefits such as health insurance and retirement savings. Employers, too, must adapt by offering more flexible work arrangements while finding ways to support and retain a diverse and geographically dispersed workforce.

The Impact of Automation and AI on Employment

The Technological Revolution

Automation and AI are poised to reshape the labour market in ways that were once the stuff of science fiction. From self-driving cars to intelligent chatbots, these technologies are automating tasks that were once the exclusive domain of human workers. While this can lead to increased efficiency and innovation, it also raises concerns about job displacement and the future of work for millions of people.

Job Displacement vs. Job Creation

The impact of automation and AI on employment is complex. While certain jobs, particularly those involving routine, manual tasks, are at risk of being automated, new opportunities are emerging in technology, data analysis, healthcare, and other fields. The challenge lies in ensuring that the workforce is prepared to transition into these new roles.

The Skills Gap

As automation and AI continue to evolve, the demand for high-tech skills will grow. Workers will need to acquire new competencies, such as data literacy, coding, and digital problem-solving, to remain competitive in the job market. Employers and educational institutions must collaborate to address the skills gap, providing training and reskilling programs that equip workers for the jobs of the future.

Ethical Considerations

The rise of AI and automation also brings ethical considerations to the forefront. Issues such as bias in AI algorithms, the impact on privacy, and the potential for increased inequality must be addressed through thoughtful regulation and corporate responsibility. Ensuring that the benefits of technological advancements are broadly shared is crucial for building a just and equitable future of work.

Preparing for the Workforce of the Future

Lifelong Learning and Adaptability

In a rapidly changing job market, adaptability is key. The workforce of the future will need to embrace lifelong learning, continuously updating skills and knowledge to keep pace with technological and economic changes. This shift requires a cultural change, where learning becomes an integral part of work and personal development.

The Role of Education and Training

Educational institutions must evolve to meet the demands of the future workforce. This includes integrating technology into curricula, offering more flexible learning options, and focusing on skills that are in high demand, such as critical thinking, creativity, and emotional intelligence. Vocational training and apprenticeships will also play a crucial role in preparing workers for technical and skilled trades.

Building Resilience in the Face of Change

Resilience will be a critical trait for both workers and organizations in the future of work. This includes financial resilience, where individuals are encouraged to save and invest for periods of uncertainty, and organizational resilience, where companies adopt agile practices that allow them to quickly respond to market shifts. Mental and emotional resilience are equally important, as the pace of change can lead to stress and burnout if not managed effectively.

Embracing Diversity and Inclusion

The future workforce will be more diverse than ever before, with a wide range of ages, backgrounds, and perspectives. Embracing diversity and inclusion is not just a moral imperative but a business necessity. Diverse teams bring different ideas and approaches, driving innovation and helping organizations better serve a global market.

Conclusion

The future of work is full of possibilities and challenges. As technology continues to advance and societal norms evolve, the traditional work models of the past will give way to more flexible, dynamic, and inclusive approaches. By understanding the trends shaping the future of work—such as remote and gig work, automation and AI, and the need for lifelong learning—individuals and organizations can better prepare for the changes ahead. The key to success in this new landscape will be adaptability, continuous learning, and a commitment to building a workforce that is resilient, diverse, and ready to meet the challenges of the future.

23.
THE FUTURE OF THE ECONOMY

As we look to the future, the global economy is poised for significant transformations driven by rapid advancements in technology, shifts in business practices, and changing social dynamics. Understanding these changes and preparing for their impact is essential for navigating the economic landscape of the coming years. This chapter explores the emerging trends that are shaping the future of the economy, the rise of the gig economy and its implications for employment, and the strategies individuals and businesses can adopt to prepare for these changes.

Emerging Trends in Technology and Business

The Role of Technology in Economic Transformation

Technology continues to be the primary driver of economic change. Innovations such as artificial intelligence (AI), blockchain, the Internet of Things (IoT), and 5G connectivity are not only reshaping industries but also creating new ones. These technologies enable greater efficiency, connectivity, and data-driven decision-making, which are becoming critical for businesses to remain competitive.

The Rise of Digital Platforms

Digital platforms like Amazon, Alibaba, and Google have transformed the way businesses operate and consumers engage in commerce. These platforms facilitate transactions on a global scale, enabling businesses of all sizes to reach new markets and customers. The power of digital platforms lies in their ability to aggregate data, optimize supply chains, and provide personalized experiences, which are increasingly important in a highly competitive global economy.

The Shift Toward Sustainability and Social Responsibility

Consumers and investors are increasingly prioritizing sustainability and social responsibility, driving businesses to adopt more ethical and environmentally friendly practices. The transition to a green economy is gaining momentum, with renewable energy, circular economy principles, and corporate social responsibility (CSR) becoming central to business strategies. This shift is not only a response to consumer demand but also a recognition of the long-term economic benefits of sustainable practices.

Globalization and Regionalization

While globalization has been a dominant force in the world economy for decades, there is a growing trend toward regionalization, driven by geopolitical tensions, trade wars, and the desire for more resilient supply chains. This shift is leading to a reconfiguration of global trade networks, with companies seeking to balance the benefits of global reach with the need for localized production and supply chain security.

The Gig Economy and Its Impact on Employment

Understanding the Gig Economy

The gig economy, characterized by short-term, flexible, and freelance work, is becoming an increasingly important part of the labour market. Platforms like Uber, TaskRabbit, and Fiverr have made it easier for individuals to find gig work, offering opportunities for supplementary income or full-time employment outside of traditional job structures.

Benefits and Challenges of the Gig Economy

The gig economy offers several benefits, including flexibility, autonomy, and the ability to earn income from multiple sources. However, it also presents challenges, such as income instability, lack of benefits like health insurance and retirement savings, and the potential for worker exploitation. The gig economy blurs the lines between employment and self-employment, raising important questions about labour rights and protections.

The Future of Work in the Gig Economy

As the gig economy continues to grow, there will be increasing pressure on governments and policymakers to address these challenges. This may involve creating new regulations that provide gig workers with access to benefits and protections traditionally reserved for full-time employees. Additionally, businesses that rely on gig workers will need to find ways to ensure fair treatment and compensation while maintaining the flexibility that makes the gig economy attractive.

Preparing for Economic Changes in the Future

Lifelong Learning and Skills Development

In an economy driven by technological change, the ability to adapt and learn new skills is crucial. Lifelong learning will become the norm as workers need to continuously update their skills to remain relevant in the job market. Educational institutions, employers, and governments must collaborate to provide accessible and affordable training programs that prepare individuals for the jobs of the future.

Building Financial Resilience

Economic changes can create uncertainty, making financial resilience more important than ever. Individuals should prioritize saving, investing, and diversifying their income sources to protect against economic downturns and job loss. This also includes planning for retirement, managing debt, and ensuring that financial goals are aligned with future economic conditions.

Embracing Flexibility and Innovation

The future economy will require a mindset that embraces flexibility and innovation. Businesses will need to be agile, constantly adapting to changing market conditions and consumer preferences. This includes adopting new technologies, exploring new business models, and fostering a culture of innovation that encourages experimentation and risk-taking.

The Role of Government and Policy

Governments will play a critical role in shaping the future economy by enacting policies that promote innovation, protect workers, and ensure economic stability. This may involve updating labour laws, investing in infrastructure, and supporting small businesses and startups. Additionally, governments will need to address the challenges posed by automation, AI, and the gig economy, ensuring that the benefits of economic growth are widely shared.

Conclusion

The future of the economy is both exciting and uncertain, shaped by powerful forces such as technology, globalization, and shifting societal values. As we move forward, individuals, businesses, and governments must work together to navigate these changes, embracing the opportunities they present while addressing the challenges they pose. By staying informed, adaptable, and proactive, we can ensure that the future economy is one that promotes prosperity, inclusivity, and sustainability for all.

APPENDIX

GLOSSARY OF ECONOMIC TERMS

A

Ability-to-pay principle

The idea that taxes should be levied on a person according to how well that person can shoulder that burden.

Adjustable-rate mortgage (ARM)

A mortgage that permits the lender to periodically adjust the interest rate on the basis of changes in a specified index.

Advertising

Communication used by businesses to persuade consumers to buy a good or service.

Algorithm

A process or set of rules to be followed in calculations or other problem-solving operations, especially by a computer.

Allocation

Ways in which to distribute goods, services or resources.

Alternatives

The different possibilities to choose from in a given situation.

Annual percentage rate (APR)

The percentage cost of credit on an annual basis and the total cost of credit to the consumer. APR combines the interest paid over the life of the loan and all fees that are paid up front.

Annuity

A series of fixed payments of the same amount paid at regular intervals (i.e., every week, month, or pay period) over a specified period of time.

Antitrust law

Legislation that prohibits practices that restrain trade, such as price fixing and business arrangements designed to achieve monopoly power.

Appreciation

An increase in value. Currency appreciation is an increase in the value of one currency relative to another.

Asset

A resource with economic value that an individual, corporation, or country owns with the expectation that it will provide future benefits.

Asymmetric information

A situation in which one party to an economic transaction has less information than the other party.

Auction

A sale of property to the highest bidder.

Automated teller machine (ATM) card

A form of debit card used in a cash machine to access an account by using a code or personal identification number.

Automation

Automatically controlled operation of an apparatus, process, or system by mechanical or electronic devices that take the place of human labour.

B

Balanced budget

Occurs when the federal government's expenditures on programs equal the amount of tax revenue collected.

Balance sheet

A statement of the assets and liabilities of a firm or individual at some given time.

Bank failure

Occurs when banks are unable to meet depositors' demands for their money.

Bank panic

Occurs when a bank run begins at one bank and spreads to others, causing people to lose confidence in banks.

Bank reserves

The amount of deposits not loaned out by banks.

Bank run

Occurs when many depositors rush to the bank to withdraw their money at the same time.

Bankruptcy

A legal process for declaring that a person is unable to pay his or her debts. The process may involve a court-supervised process of selling the bankrupt person's belongings to pay part of the debts owed to creditors.

Banks

Businesses that accept deposits and make loans.

Bank statement

A statement given to account holders by a bank or credit union to keep them informed of all transactions they made during the statement period. These statements are sent on a regular basis or posted online.

Barriers to entry

Obstacles that make it difficult for a producer to enter a market. Examples might include control of a scarce resource or high fixed or start-up costs.

Barter

Trading goods and services for other goods and services without using money.

Behavioral economics

A field in economics that uses insights from psychology and other behavioral sciences to learn how individuals make economic decisions.

GLOSSARY OF ECONOMIC TERMS

Beneficiary

The person designated to receive benefits.

Benefits

Things favorable to a decision maker; rewards gained from an action/activity.

Bond

A certificate of indebtedness issued by a government or corporation.

Bond yield

The average return from owning a bond. It depends on the price paid for the bond, its coupon payments, and time to maturity.

Boom

A period characterized by sustained increases in several economic indicators—for example, output, investment, and employment.

Borrower

An individual or business that borrows money from a lender with the expectation that they will pay the money back

Borrowing

Taking money with a promise to repay the money in the future.

Boycott

A method of protest where people show a business that they are angry by refusing to buy the goods or services it produces.

Budget
An itemized summary of probable income and expenses for a given period. A budget is a plan for managing income, spending, and saving during a given period of time.

Business
An organization that produces the goods and services that are sold to consumers in the market.

Business cycle
The fluctuating levels of economic activity in an economy over a period of time measured from the beginning of one recession to the beginning of the next.

C

Capital (financial)
The funds invested in a bank that are available to absorb loan losses or other problems and therefore protect depositors. Capital includes all equity and some types of debt. Bank regulators have developed two definitions of capital for supervisory purposes: Tier 1 capital can absorb losses while a bank continues operating. Tier 2 capital may be of limited life and may carry an interest obligation or other characteristics of a debt obligation; therefore it provides less protection to depositors than tier 1 capital.

Capital gains
A profit from the sale of financial investments.

Capital goods
See Capital resources.

GLOSSARY OF ECONOMIC TERMS

Capital investment

The purchase of physical capital goods (e.g., buildings, tools and equipment) that are used to produce goods and services.

Capital resources

Goods that have been produced and are used to produce other goods and services. They are used over and over again in the production process. Also called capital goods and physical capital.

Cash advance

A short-term loan from a bank or alternative lender that features fast approval and quick funding, but it often comes with higher fees than other options.

Cash flow

Income (dollars coming in, usually from working) minus expenses (dollars going out, usually to buy goods and services).

Central bank

An institution that oversees and regulates the banking system and quantity of money in the economy.

Certificate of deposit (CD)

A savings alternative in which money is left on deposit for a stated period of time to earn a specific interest rate.

Characteristics of money

Important features money should have. Money should be portable, durable, divisible, generally acceptable, relatively scarce, and uniform.

Check (Cheque)

A printed form directing a bank to withdraw money from an account and pay it to another account.

Checkable deposits

Deposits in accounts against which checks can be written.

Checking account

An account held at a financial institution in which account owners deposit funds. Account owners can write checks on their accounts and use ATM cards or debit cards to access funds.

Choice

A decision made between two or more possibilities or alternatives.

Closed economy

An economy that does not interact with other economies.

Coin

Money, usually minted from some combination of metals.

Coincidence of wants

Each participant in an exchange is willing to trade what he or she has in exchange for what the other participant is willing to trade.

Collateral

Property required by a lender and offered by a borrower as a guarantee of payment on a loan. Also, a borrower's savings, investments, or the value of the asset purchased that can be seized if the borrower fails to repay a debt.

Collusion

Collusion is an illegal agreement among firms to divide the market, set prices, or limit production.

Command economy

An economic system where the government owns the resources and decides what goods and services are produced, how they are produced, and who gets them. The government decides the prices of goods, services, and resources.

Commercial Bank

Businesses that accept deposits and make loans.

Commercial paper

A short-term, unsecured promissory note issued by an industrial or commercial firm, a financial company, or a foreign government. Typically, maturity is 90 to 180 days.

Commission

Monetary compensation earned for selling a particular good or service. The amount of compensation is usually related to the size of the sale.

Common stock

A share of ownership of public corporations; stockholders may vote on matters affecting the company.

Competitive markets

Markets in which there are many buyers and many sellers so that each has a negligible impact on market prices.

Compound interest

Interest computed on the sum of the original principal and accrued interest.

Consumer confidence

A measure of how consumers feel about the economy, considered an indicator of consumers' spending and saving decisions.

Consumer goods

Goods and services that are used for current consumption.

Consumer price index (CPI)

A measure of the average change over time in the prices paid by urban consumers for a market basket of consumer goods and services.

Consumers

People who buy goods and services to satisfy their wants.

Consumer sovereignty

The ability to influence what is produced and consumed in an economy through consumption activities.

Consumption

Occurs when people use goods and services.

Contraction

A period when real GDP declines; a period of economic decline.

Contractionary monetary policy

Actions taken by a central bank to increase interest rates and thereby discourage spending by consumers and businesses.

Corporation

A company owned by shareholders.

Cost of living

The amount of income needed to achieve a given living standard.

Cost-push inflation

Inflation that occurs when the costs of production (including wages and raw materials) increase, and those higher costs are passed on to consumers.

Costs of production

The amount producers pay for the resources used to produce a product.

Coverage

How much risk or liability is protected with an insurance policy.

Credit

The granting of money or something else of value in exchange for a promise of future repayment.

Credit cards

Cards that represent an agreement between a lender—the institution issuing the card—and the cardholder. Credit cards may be used repeatedly to buy products or services or to borrow money on credit. Credit cards are issued by banks, savings and loan associations, retail stores, and other businesses.

Credit history

A person's payment activity over a period of time.

Creditor

A person, financial institution, or other business that lends money.

Credit rating agencies

Firms that rate the quality of bonds and other financial securities. These ratings are used by investors to assess the probability of default. Well-known rating agencies include Moody's, Standard & Poor's, and Fitch Ratings. Firms in this business must meet standards enforced by the Securities and Exchange Commission.

Credit report

A loan and bill payment history kept by a credit bureau and used by financial institutions and other potential creditors to determine the likelihood that a future debt will be repaid.

Credit union

A nonprofit financial institution that is owned by its members.

Currency

Money, usually made from some type of paper-like material.

Cyclical unemployment

Unemployment associated with recessions in the business cycle.

D

Data mining

Analyzing large amounts of data to discover patterns.

Data robots

Software-based automated processes that complete data-related tasks, such as downloading or checking for updates.

Debit card

A plastic card similar to a credit card that allows money to be withdrawn or payments made directly from the holder's bank account.

Debits

Charges to or withdrawals from an account. In a bank account register, debits are subtracted from the balance.

Debt

Money owed in exchange for loans or for goods or services purchased with credit.

Debtor

A person or organization that owes an amount money.

Decisionmaking

Deciding among choices (alternatives or options).

Default

Default is the failure to promptly pay interest or principal when due.

Deferral

Postponed until a later time.

Deflation

A general, sustained downward movement of prices for goods and services in an economy.

Delayed gratification

The act of resisting an impulse to take an immediately available reward in the hopes of obtaining a more-valued reward. The ability to delay gratification is essential to self-regulation or self-control.

Demand

The various quantities of a good or service that buyers are willing and able to buy at all possible prices during a certain time period.

Demand curve

The graphic representation of the various quantities of a good or service that buyers are willing and able to buy at all possible prices during a certain time period.

Demographic data

Statistical data about the characteristics of a population. Examples include age, gender, and income of the people within a population.

Depository institution

A financial institution such as a savings bank, commercial bank, savings and loan association, or credit union that is legally allowed to accept monetary deposits from consumers.

Depreciation

A decrease in value. Currency depreciation is a decrease in the value of one currency relative to another.

Depression

A severe and long-lasting economic downturn that is worse and deeper than a recession; a severe reduction in gross domestic product (GDP).

Diminishing marginal utility

Occurs when marginal utility becomes smaller as a person consumes more units of a product. As someone consumes additional units of a product, the marginal utility derived from each additional unit declines.

Diminishing returns

Each additional unit of a factor of production adds less output than the one before it.

Direct deposit

An electronic transaction in which money is deposited directly into a payee's bank account from a payer's bank account.

Discouraged worker

Someone who is not working and is not looking for work because of a belief that there are no jobs available to him or her.

Discretionary income

The portion of personal income available for spending after taxes and basic essentials have been deducted.

Disposable income

The amount of a person's paycheck that is available to spend or save.

Dissaving

To consume more than income; essentially, the opposite of saving.

Diversification

Investment in various financial instruments in order to reduce risk.

Dividend

A share of a company's net profits paid to stockholders.

Division of labour

An approach to completing a complex task that breaks the project into a number of smaller, simpler tasks, which are assigned to individuals who generally perform only these duties.

Domestic

Inside a particular country.

Double coincidence of wants

Each participant in an exchange is willing to trade what he or she has in exchange for what the other participant is willing to trade.

Down payment

A sum of money is put toward the purchase price to reduce the amount of money borrowed.

Durable good

Something that lasts at least three years, such as a home appliance or an automobile.

E

Earned income

Earned income is the money you get for the work you do. There are two ways to get earned income: You work for someone who pays you or you own or run a business or farm.

Earnings

Money or income received in exchange for labour or scrviccs.

Economic efficiency

Answers the question, "How well are productive resources (land, labour, capital, and entrepreneurial ability) being allocated?" Economic efficiency involves both producing the goods and services that people want and using inputs in a way that keeps production costs as low as possible.

Economic equality

A more equal distribution of goods and services to citizens. Also known as economic equity.

Economic equity

A more equal distribution of goods and services to citizens. Also known as economic equality.

Economic freedom

Answers the question, "Do I get to decide where to live, what job to have, how to spend and save my money, and so on?" Economic freedom means allowing students to choose career paths, workers to change jobs and join unions, consumers to choose how to spend and save their money, people to start businesses and close businesses, people to travel as they wish to, and so on.

Economic growth

A sustained rise over time in a nation's production of goods and services.

Economic indicator

Statistical data used to determine the health of the economy.

Economic interdependence

A condition that results when economic agents (people, regions, countries) specialize in the production of particular goods and services based on available resources and skills, and then trade with others to obtain other desired goods and services.

Economic models

Simple depictions of complex ideas.

Economics

The everyday business of life. A social science that studies the decisions people make when faced with scarce resources. In particular, economics is about decisions related to the production, distribution, and consumption of goods and services.

Economic stability

Answers the question, "How do we keep the economy stable so that people feel secure and can plan?" Economic stability means maintaining stable prices and full employment and keeping economic growth reasonably smooth and steady. Price stability means avoiding inflation or deflation. Full employment occurs when an economy's scarce resources, especially labor, are fully utilized.

Economic wants

Desires that can be satisfied by consuming goods and services. Also known as wants.

Economies of scale

Factors that cause a producer's average cost per unit to fall as output rises.

Economy

A system of production and distribution of resources, goods, and services.

Educational attainment

Highest level of education a student completes (high school, college, graduate).

Elastic demand

The type of demand that exists when the percentage change in quantity demanded is greater than the percentage change in price; that is, consumers are very sensitive to a change in the price of a good or service.

Embargo

A government order that limits or prohibits trade with a particular country or group of countries.

Emissions tax

Firms can pollute as much as they would like as long as they pay the tax for each unit of pollution.

Employed

People 16 years and older who have jobs.

Employee

A person who works for an employer in exchange for a monetary payment.

Employer

A person or business providing a job or work to others and giving a monetary payment in exchange for the work.

Employment rate

The percentage of the labour force that is employed.

Energy

Fuel used to power the economy. Energy is harvested from nonrenewable resources such as fossil fuels (natural gas, coal, oil) or renewable resources such as solar, wind, or geothermal heat.

Entrepreneurs

Individuals who are willing to take risks in order to develop new products and start new businesses. They recognize opportunities, enjoy working for themselves, and accept challenges.

Entrepreneurship

A characteristic of people who assume the risk of organizing productive resources to produce goods and services.

Equilibrium price

The price at which quantity supplied and quantity demanded are equal. The point at which the supply and demand curves intersect.

Equilibrium wage

The wage at which the quantity of labour supplied and quantity of labour demanded are equal.

Equity

The difference between the value of an asset and what is owed on the asset.

Excess reserves

Amount of funds held by a depository institution in its account at a Federal Reserve Bank in excess of its required reserve balance and its contractual clearing balance.

Exchange

Trading goods and services with people for other goods and services or for money.

Exchange rate

The price of one country's currency in terms of another country's currency.

Exempt property

Property a debtor is allowed to keep when filing for bankruptcy.

Expansion

A period when real GDP increases; a period of economic growth.

Expansionary monetary policy

Actions taken by a central bank to lower interest rates and thereby encourage spending by consumers and businesses.

Expected rate of return

The amount you anticipate receiving on an investment based on the probable rates of return (often based on how the asset performed in the past).

Expenditures

Money spent to buy goods and services.

Expenses

The costs people incur for goods and services. Expenses are often categorized as fixed, variable, and periodic. Fixed expenses are those that occur each month in a regular amount, such as rent, car payments, and mortgage payments. Variable expenses are those that change from one time period to the next, such as food, clothing, gasoline, and entertainment. Periodic expenses are those that occur several times a year, such as car insurance and life insurance payments.

Explicit cost

A cost that involves actually laying out money. A direct expense that a business incurs, such as rent, salaries, wages, or utility bills.

Exports

Resources, goods, and services that are produced domestically but sold abroad. Exports are sent into a region from outside that region.

External costs

Happen when a person does something that benefits himself or herself that unintentionally makes another person worse off.

Externality

A cost or benefit to a third party arising from a transaction between two parties unrelated to the third party.

F

Face value (of bond)

The value printed on the face of a stock, bond, or other financial instrument or document.

Factors of production

The natural, human, and capital resources that are available to make goods and services. Also known as productive resources.

Federal Reserve System

The central bank system of the United States.

Fiat money

A substance or device used as money, having no intrinsic value (no value of its own), or representational value (not representing anything of value, such as gold).

Final goods and services

Goods and services sold to end users and have been purchased for final use and not for resale or further processing.

Financial institution

A business that provides services to make deposits to or withdrawals from an account, take out a loan, invest, or exchange currency.

Financial intermediary

A business that acts as the middleman between two parties in a financial transaction. Examples include commercial banks, investment banks, mutual funds and pension funds.

Financial investment

Placing money in a savings account or in any number of financial assets, such as stocks, bonds, or mutual funds, with the intention of making a financial gain.

Financial literacy

Having knowledge of financial matters and applying that knowledge to one's life.

GLOSSARY OF ECONOMIC TERMS

Financial system

The set of institutions, such as banks, insurance companies, and stock exchanges, that permit the exchange of funds.

Fiscal agent

A person or organization serving as another's financial representative.

Fiscal policy

Spending and taxing policies of the government to influence the economy.

Fixed costs

Business costs, such as rent, that are constant whatever the quantity of goods or services the business produces.

Flexible exchange rate

A system in which supply and demand determine exchange rates.

Foreclose

To take possession of a mortgaged property as a result of the borrower's failure to make mortgage payments.

Foreclosure

The legal process by which a property that is mortgaged as security for a loan may be sold and the proceeds of the sale applied to the mortgage debt. A foreclosure can occur when the loan becomes delinquent because payments have not been made or when the borrower is in default for a reason other than the failure to make timely mortgage payments.

Foreign exchange market

A market in which one country's currency can be used to purchase another country's currency.

Four-firm concentration ratio

The market share held by the four largest firms in an industry. Larger concentration ratios generally indicate less competition. The maximum value for concentration ratios is 100%.

Fractional reserve banking system

A banking system in which the amount of reserves that banks hold is less than the value of their customers' deposits.

Free rider

A person who receives benefits from something for which he or she doesn't pay.

Frictional unemployment

Unemployment that results when people are new to the job market (for example, recent graduates) or are transitioning from one job to another.

Full employment

The lowest possible unemployment rate in a growing economy with all factors of production used as efficiently as possible.

Full-time employment

Although defined by the U.S. Bureau of Labour Statistics as employment of 35 hours or more in a week, the matter of "full-time employment" is generally determined by the employer.

GLOSSARY OF ECONOMIC TERMS

Functions of money

Activities that can be carried out through the use of money. Activities include medium of exchange, unit of account, and store of value.

G

Gainful employment

A job, especially one taken after graduation, that is suited to the ability and potentiality of the one employed.

Generally acceptable (money)

An item that people will take as payment for their work or as payment for goods and services.

Gini coefficient

A statistical measure of income inequality that ranges from 0 to 1. A Gini coefficient of 1 indicates perfect income inequality, where one person earns all the income and the rest of the population earns none. Conversely, a Gini coefficient of 0 indicates that total income is equally distributed among the entire population. A Gini coefficient, at a particular point in time, can be calculated graphically by finding the area between the line representing a country's income distribution (known as the Lorenz curve) and a line of perfect income equality.

Goods

Objects that satisfy people's wants.

Government debt

The sum of accumulated budget deficits. Also known as national debt.

Government expenditures

Purchases by government of goods and services, as well as transfer payments made by government. Government expenditures are part of a government's budget.

Government securities

Bonds, notes, and other debt instruments sold by a government to finance its expenditures.

Government spending

Spending by all levels of government on goods and services. This includes, for example, spending on the military, schools, and highways. Government spending is a component of gross domestic product and does not include transfer payments.

Gross domestic product (GDP)

The total market value, expressed in dollars, of all final goods and services produced in an economy in a given year.

Gross income

The total amount earned before any adjustments are subtracted.

Gross pay

The amount people earn per pay period before any deductions or taxes are paid.

GLOSSARY OF ECONOMIC TERMS

Gross private investment

Spending by businesses on machinery, factories, equipment, tools, and construction of new buildings.

H

Hard skills

Specific, teachable abilities such as math, reading, writing, typing, and so on.

Health insurance

Insurance that pays for medical and surgical expenses incurred by the insured.

Homeowner's equity

The owner's interest in a property, calculated as the current fair market value of the property less the amount of existing liens. The appraised, or carrying value, of a property minus the amount of existing liens.

Household

A group of people living in the same home, regardless of their relationship to one another.

Housing market

The market for buying homes. Housing is often an indicator for the overall health of the economy.

Human capital

The knowledge and skills that people obtain through education, experience, and training.

Human resources

The quantity and quality of human effort directed toward producing goods and services. Also known as labour.

Hyperinflation

A very rapid rise in the overall price level; an extremely high rate of inflation.

I

Identity theft

A form of stealing that results in someone gaining access to another person's personal information (such as name, address, driver's license number, credit card numbers, date of birth, birthplace, or Social Security number) to commit all or any of the following crimes: gaining access to bank accounts to steal money, making purchases with credit or debit cards, opening credit, or engaging in other criminal behaviour.

Implicit cost

An indirect cost that does not require an outlay of money; it is measured by the value, in dollar terms, of forgone benefits.

Imports

Resources, goods, and services that are produced abroad but sold domestically. Imports are brought into a region from outside a region.

Incentives

Perceived benefits that encourage certain behaviours.

GLOSSARY OF ECONOMIC TERMS

Income

The payment people receive for providing resources in the marketplace. When people work, they provide human resources (labour) and in exchange, they receive income in the form of wages or salaries. People also earn income in the forms of rent, profit, and interest.

Income distribution

The way income is distributed among individuals in a society.

Income tax

Taxes on income, both earned (salaries, wages, tips, commissions) and unearned (interest, dividends). Income taxes can be levied on both individuals (personal income taxes) and businesses (business and corporate income taxes).

Index number

A number used to represent the change in value of a magnitude (frequently of price levels) between the base date and a different date. Indices typically have a value of 100 on the base date.

Inefficiency

A condition that results when the production of goods and services involves wasted resources or when it is possible to reallocate resources in a way that would generate greater consumer satisfaction.

Inelastic demand

The type of demand that exists when the percentage change in quantity demanded is less than the percentage change in price; that is, consumers are not very sensitive to a change in the price of a good or service.

Inflation

A general, sustained upward movement of prices for goods and services in an economy.

Inflation rate

The percentage increase in the average price level of goods and services over a period of time.

Infrastructure

Basic structures, including buildings and facilities such as roads, bridges, and waste disposal systems.

Inputs

Materials and resources used to produce goods and services.

Installment credit

A loan given in a lump sum for a specific purchase or investment. The loan is paid back with regularly scheduled payments, which include interest. Examples include home loans, car loans, or business loans.

Institutions

A self-sustaining system of shared beliefs about how parties interact.

Insurance

Protection from specified losses in return for a fee (premium).

Interest

The price of using someone else's money. When people place their money in a bank, the bank uses the money to make loans to others. In return, the bank pays interest to the account holder. Those who borrow from banks or other organizations pay interest for the use of the money borrowed.

Interest rate

The percentage of the amount of a loan that is charged for a loan. Also, the percentage paid on a savings account.

Interest rate effect

The effect on consumer spending and investment spending caused by a change in the aggregate price level on the purchasing power of consumers' and firms' money holdings.

Intermediary

One who stands between two parties to facilitate a transaction; a mediator.

Intermediate good

A man-made good that is used to produce another good or service, becoming part of that good or service.

International trade

Trade between different countries.

Inventory

Goods that have been produced but remain unsold.

Investment

The purchase of physical capital goods (e.g., buildings, tools, and equipment) that are used to produce goods and services.

Investment (financial)

An asset purchased with the hope that it will gain value and provide a financial return.

Investment in human capital

The efforts people put forth to acquire human capital. These efforts include education, experience, and training.

Investors

People of institutions who provide money or other assets to a company in return for possible financial gain in the future.

J

Job

A collection of tasks grouped together similarly in a number of similar positions in a given organization.

Job enlargement

The combining of various operations at a similar level into one job to provide more variety for workers.

Job enrichment

Providing a job with more challenge, meaning, autonomy, and responsibility.

Job specification

A description of the skills and abilities necessary to perform a particular job.

K

Keynesian multiplier effect

An effect where an increase (or decrease) in a component of aggregate expenditure (i.e., consumption, investment, or government spending) produces an increase (or decrease) in national income that is greater than the initial increase (or decrease) in the component. This greater-than-proportional change in national income is the result of chain reactions that generate more (or less) activity than the original increase (or decrease).

L

Labour

The quantity and quality of human effort directed toward producing goods and services. Also known as human resources.

Labour force

The total number of workers, including both the employed and the unemployed.

Labour force participation rate

The number of people who are either employed or are actively looking for work, usually expressed as a percentage.

Labour market

The exchange of labour by workers who want to sell labour and businesses that want to purchase labour. (Also known as the job market).

Lags

The time between the recognition of an economic problem, the negotiation and implementation of a solution, and the realization of results in the economy.

Land

Things that occur naturally in and on the earth that are used to produce goods and services. Examples include oceans, air, mineral deposits, virgin forests, and actual fields of land.

Law of demand

As the price of a good or service rises, the quantity demanded of that good or service falls. Likewise, as the price of a good or service falls, the quantity demanded of that good or service rises.

Law of supply

As the price of a good or service rises, the quantity supplied of that good or service rises. Likewise, as the price of a good or service falls, the quantity supplied of that good or service falls.

Lease

A contract that states the terms and conditions a landlord and a tenant agree to regarding rental property, including payment terms, the responsibilities of both parties, and consequences if terms and conditions are not met, to ensure that both parties of the lease are protected.

Lender

An individual or organization that provides money to a borrower with the expectation that the borrower will pay the money back.

Liability

A legal responsibility to pay back money from a loan or other type of debt.

Liquid asset

An asset that is easily convertible to cash with relatively little loss of value in the conversion process.

Liquidation

The sale of a debtor's nonexempt property and the distribution of the proceeds to creditors. Chapter 7 of the U.S. Bankruptcy Code provides for the liquidation of the filer's assets and distribution of the proceeds to the filer's creditors.

Liquidity

The quality that makes an asset easily convertible into cash with relatively little loss of value in the conversion process.

Loan

A sum of money provided temporarily on the condition that the amount borrowed be repaid, usually with interest.

Loanable funds

Money made available to borrowers through the actions of savers.

L

Macroeconomics

The study of the broad economy, such as how an economy grows and how growth is maintained.

Manufacture

To make or process goods, especially in large quantities and by means of industrial machines.

Marginal benefits

The additional satisfaction a consumer receives by consuming an additional unit of a good or service.

Marginal costs

The additional cost of producing an additional unit.

Marginal satisfaction/marginal utility

The extra satisfaction from consuming 1 more unit of some good or service.

Market (marketplace)

Buyers and sellers coming together to exchange goods, services, and/or resources.

Market economy

An economic system in which decisions about what goods and services are produced, how they are produced, and who gets them are made by buyers and sellers who meet to exchange goods, services, and resources. The buyers and sellers decide the prices of goods, services, and resources.

Market power

The ability of a single economic agent (or small group of agents) to have a substantial influence on market prices.

Market price

The price at which buyers and sellers trade a good or service in the marketplace where the quantity demanded equals the quantity supplied. Also known as the market clearing price or the equilibrium price.

Maturity (of bonds)

The period during which a bond makes coupon payments. At maturity, the face value of the bond is paid. Maturity may be expressed as years, months, or weeks.

Medium of exchange

Anything that is generally acceptable in exchange for goods and services.

Menu costs

The costs to a firm incurred as a result of changing prices. The term comes from the cost incurred for printing new menus when a restaurant raises prices.

Microeconomics

The study of the markets that make up the broad economy.

Minimum wage

The lowest wage that employers may legally pay for an hour of labour.

Mixed economy

An economic system where some decisions about what is produced, how it is produced, who gets what is produced, and prices of what is produced are made by buyers and sellers. Some decisions about what is produced, how it is produced, who gets what is produced, and prices of what is produced are determined by the government.

Monetary policy

Central bank actions involving the use of interest rate or money supply tools to achieve such goals as maximum employment and stable prices.

Monetary transmission

How monetary policy-induced changes in the policy rate impact economic variables such as aggregate output, employment, and inflation.

Money

Anything widely accepted in exchange for goods and services.

Money creation

An increase in the money supply generated by the banking system through the lending of reserves.

Money multiplier

In a fractional-reserve system, the maximum amount of money (deposits) the banking system generates through lending from each additional dollar of reserves.

Money neutrality

An economic theory stating that, in the long run, changes in the money supply cause changes in variables, such as price and wages, but not in unemployment or real (or inflation-adjusted) variables, such as real GDP (gross domestic product) and real consumption.

Money supply

The quantity of money available in an economy. The basic money supply consists of currency, coins, and checking account (demand) deposits. Also known as money stock.

Monopolistic competition

A market structure where many firms produce similar but not identical products.

Monopoly

A market for a good or service where there is only one supplier, or that is dominated by one supplier. Barriers prevent entry to the market and there are no close substitutes for the product.

Monopsony

A market for a good or service where there is only one buyer, or that is dominated by one buyer.

Moral hazard

The risk that one party to a transaction will engage in behavior that is undesirable from the other party's view.

Mortgage

A loan for the purchase of a home or real estate.

Mortgage debt

A debt owed for loans for homes and real estate.

Multiplier

A factor of proportionality that measures how much an endogenous variable changes in response to a change in an exogenous variable. Some examples include the government spending multiplier, the money multiplier, and the Keynesian multiplier.

Mutual fund

A company that pools investors' money and then issues shares to its investors.

N

National debt

The accumulation of budget deficits. Also known as government debt.

Natural rate of unemployment

The unemployment rate that stems from economic factors unrelated to changes in aggregate demand. The rate of unemployment that does not contain cyclical unemployment.

Natural resources

Things that occur naturally in and on the earth that are used to produce goods and services.

Negative externality

A negative side effect that results when the production or consumption of a good or service affects the welfare of people who are not the parties directly involved in a market exchange.

Negative incentive

A penalty that discourages people from behaving in a certain way.

Nest egg

An amount of money saved for a special occasion, such as retirement or buying a house.

Net exports

A component of gross domestic product (GDP), net exports are the result of exports minus imports.

Net pay

Gross pay minus deductions and taxes.

Net worth

The value of a person's assets minus the value of his or her liabilities.

Nominal

Monetary values measured in current prices.

Nominal gross domestic product

The total market value of all final goods and services produced in an economy in a given year, expressed using the current year's price for goods and services. Also known as current-dollar GDP.

Nominal value

A monetary value measured in current prices.

Nondurable good

Something that lasts less than three years, such as food or clothing.

O

Oligopoly

A market structure in which a few large firms (sellers) dominate a market.

Online banking

An electronic payment system that allows customers of a bank or credit union to conduct a wide variety of financial transactions through the bank or credit union website or app.

Open market operations

The buying and selling of government securities through primary dealers by the central bank. When the securities are bought or sold, reserves in the banking system are increased or decreased, respectively.

Opportunity cost

The value of the next-best alternative when a decision is made; it's what is given up.

Option

A contract to buy or sell a specific financial product known as the underlying instrument at a pre-specified price.

Outputs

Goods and services that are produced.

P

Paradox of thrift

A controversial Keynesian economics theory that proposes that if everyone tries to save more during a recession, aggregate demand will fall. As a result, the theory argues everyone would grow poorer instead of richer because of the decreases in aggregate consumption and economic growth.

Patent

A license that gives the inventor of a new product the exclusive right to sell it for a specific period of time.

Payday loan

A small, short-term loan that is intended to cover a borrower's expenses until his or her next payday. May also be called a paycheck advance or a payday advance.

Payroll deduction

Amounts subtracted from gross pay.

Per capita

Per person. Determined by dividing the total quantity by the total population.

Per capita gross domestic product

Gross domestic product (GDP) divided by the total population of a country.

Per capita measure

The same as an average-person or a mean-person measure.

Per capita personal income

The total income earned by individuals in a state, region, or country during a year, divided by the population of the state, region, or country.

Perfect competition

A market in which there are many buyers and many sellers of an identical product.

Personal consumption expenditures

A measurement of goods and services purchased by residents.

Personal identification number (PIN)

A required code known only by the cardholder that is used to make transactions; the PIN is entered into a terminal and sent to an authorizing entity to verify the account.

Personal income

The income that individuals receive from all sources, including wages and salaries, dividends and interest, rents, profits, and transfer payments.

Personal saving rate

The ratio of personal saving to disposable personal income; the fraction of income, after taxes, that is saved.

Phillips Curve

An economic model indicating an inverse relationship between the rate of inflation and the rate of unemployment.

Physical capital

Goods that have been produced and are used to produce other goods and services. They are used over and over again in the production process. Also called capital goods and capital resources.

Point-of-sale (POS) terminal

An electronic device for the acceptance of payment cards; POS refers to the area or location where customers can pay for their purchases.

Policy lags

The time between the recognition of an economic problem, the negotiation and implementation of a solution, and the realization of results in the economy.

Portable

Easy to carry.

Portfolio

A list or collection of financial assets that an individual or company holds.

Positive externality

A benefit to a third party arising from a transaction between two parties unrelated to the third party.

Potential GDP

The real output an economy can produce when it fully employs its available resources.

Potential output

The real output (GDP) an economy can produce when it fully employs its available resources.

Preferences

An indication of our likes or dislikes; preferences help us make choices.

Price

The amount of money, determined by the interaction of buyers and sellers, that a buyer must pay to acquire a good, service, or resource.

Price ceiling

A government-mandated maximum price that can be charged for a good or service.

Price controls

A restriction on a market that sets the price above or below the market equilibrium.

Price discrimination

The practice of selling the same good or service at different prices to different customers.

Price floor

A government-mandated minimum price that must be paid for a good or service.

Principal

The original amount of money deposited or invested, excluding any interest or dividends. Also refers to the original amount of a loan without any interest.

Private good

A good that once used by one person cannot be used by someone else. They are considered rival in consumption and/or excludable. A person can be excluded from using a private good.

Producer price index (PPI)

A measure of the change over time in the prices received by producers of goods and services.

Producers

People who make goods and services.

Production

The process of using resources and intermediate goods to make goods and provide services.

Production function

The combination of inputs to produce outputs.

Production possibilities frontier

A graphic representation of output combinations that can be produced given an economy's available resources and technology.

Productive capacity

The maximum output an economy can produce with the current level of available resources.

Productive resources

The natural, human, and capital resources used to make goods and services. Also known as factors of production.

Productivity

The ratio of output per worker per unit of time.

Profit

The amount of revenue that remains after a business pays the costs of producing a good or service.

Progressive Tax

A tax in which high-income earners pay a larger fraction of their income in taxes than low-income earners do.

Property rights

The legal ownership of something with economic value.

Proportional (Flat) Tax

A taxing system that takes the same percentage of tax at all income levels.

Public good

A good that is non-rival and non-excludable. Use by one person does not prevent its consumption by others.

Purchasing power

The amount of goods and services that a unit of currency can buy.

Q

Quantitative easing (QE)

A monetary policy in which a central bank makes large-scale asset purchases designed to bolster financial market conditions.

Quantity demanded

The amount of a good or service that consumers are willing and able to buy at a specific price.

GLOSSARY OF ECONOMIC TERMS

Quantity supplied

The amount of a good or service that businesses are willing and able to sell at a specific price.

Quantity theory of money

A theory that emphasizes the relationship between the money supply and the price level.

Quota

A limit on the quantity of a good that can come into a country.

R

Rate of return

A useful measure to compare how different assets may increase your wealth.

Real

Monetary values, wages, or prices, adjusted for inflation and measured in constant prices—that is, in prices of a given or base period. Real monetary values are obtained by adjusting nominal wages or prices with a price measure such as the CPI.

Real asset

A tangible item that has intrinsic value because of its substance and properties.

Real gross domestic product (GDP)

The total market value of all final goods and services produced in an economy in a given year calculated by using a base year's price for goods and services; nominal gross domestic product (GDP) adjusted for inflation.

Real interest rate

The price of borrowed money, adjusted for inflation.

Real rate of return

The rate of return on the investment minus the inflation rate.

Real value

A measure of money that removes the effect of inflation.

Recession

A period of declining real income and rising unemployment. A significant decline in general economic activity extending over a period of time.

Recycle

To collect used materials and use them to produce new goods.

Regressive Tax

A taxing system that takes a larger percentage of a lower income and a lower percentage of a higher income.

Rent

The payment for natural resources.

Rent controls

A type of price control that typically sets the rental rate for an apartment below the market rate.

Repossess

To retake possession of something when the buyer fails to make payments.

GLOSSARY OF ECONOMIC TERMS

Reserve requirement

The percentage of a bank's deposits that it is required to keep on hand (in the form of either reserve balances or vault cash).

Resources

The natural, capital, and human resources used to produce goods and services. Also known as productive resources.

Retail

The resale of new and used goods to general consumers.

Retained earnings

A portion of a company's profit used as savings, to pay off debt, or to reinvest in the company.

Retirement

Permanently leaving a job, career, occupation, or active working life.

Return on Investment (ROI)

A performance measure of the effectiveness of an investment. ROI is calculated as the net gain (gain from investment minus cost of investment) divided by the cost of investment.

Revenue

Money received; income.

Revolving credit

A line of available credit that is usually designed to be used repeatedly, with a preapproved credit limit. The amount of available credit decreases and increases as funds are borrowed and then repaid with interest.

Risk

The chance of loss.

Risk averse

An investor who will trade off a higher return for the benefit of greater certainty of return.

Rule of 72

A method to estimate the number of years it will take for a financial investment (or debt) to double its value (or cost). Divide 72 by the interest rate (percentage) to determine the approximate number of years it will take the investment (debt) to double its value (cost).

S

Salary

Income earned for providing human resources (labour) in the market. Salaries are generally an annual amount paid monthly or bimonthly for a specified number of hours, usually 40 hours per week.

Save

To keep money to spend in the future.

Saving

Income not spent on current consumption or taxes. Saving involves giving up some current consumption for future consumption.

GLOSSARY OF ECONOMIC TERMS

Saving rate

The percentage of your income that you save.

Savings

The accumulation of money set aside for future spending.

Savings account

An account with a bank or credit union in which people can deposit their money for future use and earn interest.

Savings and loan associations

Financial institutions that accept savings deposits and invest the bulk of those deposits in mortgages.

Savings goal

A good or service that you want to buy in the future.

Savings plan

A schedule listing tasks that, when completed, will allow a saver to reach a savings goal.

Scarcity

The condition that exists because there are not enough resources to produce everyone's wants.

Seasonally adjusted

Data adjusted mathematically to remove the ups and downs that occur due to seasonal events, such as extra retail workers hired for the holidays. Seasonal adjustment removes the effects of events that follow a more or less regular pattern each year. These adjustments make it easier to observe the cyclical and other nonseasonal movements in a data series.

Seasonal unemployment

Unemployment caused by changes in the weather or seasons.

Secured loan

A loan that is backed with collateral; a loan for which the lender requires and the borrower offers property as a guarantee of repayment.

Security deposit

Money paid by a tenant to a landlord that the landlord holds during the occupancy and may use to pay for any damage or unpaid rent when the lease ends or must otherwise return to the tenant. State laws dictate how soon it must be repaid after the lease ends.

Services

Actions that can satisfy people's wants.

Shoe-leather costs

The figurative costs of replacing shoes more often because of increased trips to the bank. This would occur during times of inflation when there is a real cost associated with holding currency in non-interest-bearing checking accounts.

Shortage

The condition that exists when the quantity demanded of a good or service exceeds the quantity supplied at a particular price.

Signal

A way to reveal credible information to another party.

GLOSSARY OF ECONOMIC TERMS

Simple interest

Interest paid or earned based on only the principal of a loan or account.

Sit-in

A type of protest where people refuse to buy the business's goods and services and block others from making purchases by taking all of the seats in a restaurant or blocking the entrance to a business.

Soft skills

Interpersonal skills such as communication (verbal, written), teamwork, dependability, problem-solving, leadership, time management, creativity, and so on.

Solvency

The ability of a company to meet its long-term debts and financial obligations and ultimately stay in business.

Specialization

Limiting production to fewer goods and services than consumed, perhaps those whose production entails the lower opportunity cost.

Spending

Using some or all of your income to buy things you want now.

Spread

The difference in value between two prices, interest rates, or yields.

Stagflation
The condition of relatively high inflation and relatively high unemployment occurring simultaneously.

Standard of living
A measure of the goods and services available to each person in a country; a measure of economic well-being. Also known as per capita real GDP (gross domestic product).

Stigma
A stain on one's reputation; a mark or token of disgrace.

Stimulus
Actions taken by a government or a central bank that are intended to encourage economic activity and growth.

Stock
A share of ownership in a company. Stocks are often traded publicly.

Store of value
The ability to retain worth.

Structural unemployment
Long-term joblessness caused by a mismatch in the skills held by those looking for work and the skills demanded by those seeking workers.

Subsidized loan
A loan in which the government pays the interest on the loan for a specific time.

GLOSSARY OF ECONOMIC TERMS

Subsidy

A payment made by the government to support a business or market. No good or service is provided in return for the payment.

Substitute

A similar good. With substitutes, a change in the price of one and the demand for the other tend to move in the same direction.

Sunk cost

A cost that has already been incurred and cannot be recovered.

Supply

The various quantities of a good or service that producers are willing and able to sell at all possible prices during a certain time period.

Supply curve

The graphic representation of the various quantities of a good or service that producers are willing and able to sell at all possible prices during a certain time period.

Surplus

When the quantity supplied of a good or service exceeds the quantity demanded at a particular price.

T

Tariff

A tax that must be paid before a good may be brought into a country.

Taxable income

Adjusted gross income minus allowable tax exemptions, deductions, and credits; the amount of income that is subject to income tax.

Tax base

The dollar value of something such as income, property, or an amount spent for a good or service.

Tax credit

An amount directly deducted from the total tax owed.

Taxes

Mandatory payments individuals, households, and businesses make to local, state, or national governments.

Technological advance

An advance in overall knowledge in a specific area; also known as technological change.

Technological change

See technological advance.

Total revenue

The selling price multiplied by the quantity demanded.

Trade

The exchange of resources, goods, or services for other resources, goods or services, or for money.

Trade barrier - government imposed

Any action government takes to make trade more difficult. Trade barrier - natural

GLOSSARY OF ECONOMIC TERMS

Trade deficit

The difference that results when the value of a country's imports exceeds the value of its exports.

Trade-off

Giving up some of one thing in order to gain some of something else.

Trade surplus

The difference that results when the value of a country's exports exceeds the value of its imports.

Transaction costs

The costs associated with buying or selling a good, service, or financial asset.

Transfer payments

Payments by governments to people who do not supply goods, services, or labour in exchange for the payments.

Treasury bill

A security issued by the Treasury with an original maturity of no more than one year. Interest on a Treasury bill is the difference between the purchase price and the value paid at redemption.

U

Underemployed

Wanting a full-time job but having only a part-time job; being overqualified for a job and receiving less pay than would be earned at a job requiring a higher skill level.

Unemployment

A condition where people at least 16 years old are without jobs and actively seeking work.

Unemployment rate

The percentage of the labour force that is willing and able to work, does not currently have a job, and is actively looking for employment.

Unit of account

A common measurement used to compare the value of goods and services.

Unsecured loan

A loan not backed with collateral.

Utility/Satisfaction

The total satisfaction received from consuming goods and services.

V

Value

The amount of satisfaction or happiness that a good or service gives an individual.

Variable costs

Costs that change as the quantity of goods and services that a business produces changes.

Volatile

Likely to change in a sudden or extreme way.

Volatility

A sudden or large change in the price of an asset.

Volunteering

Performing an activity, task, or service for another person or organization without being paid.

W

Wage garnishment

A court order imposed on an employer to withhold a portion of an employee's wages to be sent to a person or business to whom the employee owes money.

Wage inflation

A general, sustained upward movement in the average level of wages.

Wages

Income earned for providing human resources (labor) in the market. Wages are usually computed by multiplying an hourly pay rate by the number of hours worked.

Wants

Desires that can be satisfied by consuming goods and services.

Waste

The unavoidable material that remains after something has been consumed or produced.

Wealth

The value of a person's assets accumulated over time minus liabilities.

Wholesale

The selling of goods in large quantities to be retailed by others.

Withdrawal

A sum of money taken out of an account.

Y

Yield

The average return from owning a bond. Yield depends on the price paid for the bond, its coupon payments, and the time to maturity.

Yield curve

A graph that shows the yields of bonds with different maturity dates.

www.ingramcontent.com/pod-product-compliance
Lightning Source LLC
Chambersburg PA
CBHW070546010526
44118CB00012B/1241